The Greater City

NEW YORK, 1898-1948

Brown Brothers

PUBLISHED 1948 IN NEW YORK

Brown Brothers

The Greater City

NEW YORK, 1898–1948

Edited by Allan Nevins and John A. Krout

COLUMBIA UNIVERSITY PRESS

Foreword

MAYOR WILLIAM O'DWYER, on May 5, 1947, appointed the Mayor's Committee for the Commemoration of the Golden Anniversary of the City of New York. The Mayor charged the Committee with the preparation and execution of plans to commemorate adequately the fifty-year period since the consolidation in 1898 of the boroughs of Manhattan, Brooklyn, the Bronx, Queens, and Richmond, into the Greater City of New York. The Mayor also directed that an authentic history be written of this period by recognized historians. Professors Allan Nevins and John A. Krout of Columbia University were commissioned to do this work and Columbia University Press was engaged to publish the book. These two eminent historians, enlisting the aid of the writers represented on these pages, have compiled a volume which graphically portrays the half-century of history and progress between 1898 and 1948, and also captures the color and spirit of this vital cosmopolitan center, idealistic and tolerant, yet practical and realistic. In this chronicle, with all of its human drama, can be found the success of the City of New York in achieving a more democratic government, a stronger economy, and a deeper culture.

As we pay tribute to this Fiftieth Anniversary of the City of Greater New York, I cordially commend this volume, comprehensive in scope and rich in pictorial content, not only to the residents of the five boroughs, but also to all Americans and other friends who join with us in this Golden Anniversary commemoration of the Greater City of New York.

Grover A. Whalen
CHAIRMAN

Contents

Wide World

Past, Present, and Future

By ALLAN NEVINS

WHEN Greater New York was brought into being under the guidance of Andrew H. Green, Benjamin F. Tracy, Seth Low, and other farsighted leaders, the city was the metropolis of the United States. Fifty years later it might almost call itself the world metropolis. Down to the first World War, it had yielded precedence in financial fields to London, in artistic fields to Paris, and in musical fields to Berlin. In the period between wars these European capitals had struggled bravely to regain their old position. But at the end of the second World War New York stood alone. Even in population, London, which had kept abreast of it only by annexing outlying suburbs, was ready to yield first place to its eight millions. In wealth, resources, and volume of hopeful energy no city of battered, impoverished Europe, of adolescent Latin America, or of the interior United States, could challenge its primacy.

As its downtown skyscrapers had no equals abroad, so the banking houses in their shadow settled the financial destinies of the planet. Its universities and technical schools had richer equipment and greater armies of students than those of any other center. Its workshops and ateliers displayed a skill second to those of no other city. It was a lodestone ceaselessly attracting the best brains and talent in business, the profes-

STREET SCENES, 1898

sions, and the arts. Its publishing houses issued more books, and its newspapers and magazines poured forth a greater flood of information, than those of any other capital. It was the greatest theatrical center on the globe. New Yorkers knew that their city had countless faults and shortcomings, that they had much to deplore as well as much to boast. Nevertheless, here were more power, energy, skill, and aspiration than were gathered in any other community of the world. It was a fitting spot in which to place the home of the United Nations.

But was this gigantic agglomeration really a unified city? For some time after the annexation of the East Bronx in 1895 and the merger with Brooklyn, Queens, and Richmond in 1898, that question might have inspired an emphatic nega-

[2]

tive. In the mid-nineteenth century, when New York was simply Manhattan, the New Yorkers had loved their city as a whole. Aware of its unique qualities—its cosmopolitan outlook, complexity of social institutions, and vitality—they had exulted in its variety, cheery energy, and color. Then, as after 1898 it became a giant among cities, with five equal boroughs, it ceased to inspire the kind of intimate affection which Washington Irving had felt when he wrote the Salmagundi Papers, or Walt Whitman when he hymned Mannahata's spires. It suddenly became too huge and multiform, it seemed, for even a lifelong resident to understand and appreciate. Moreover, the proportion of those who were born in New York seemed to become smaller and smaller. New Yorkers

[3]

GOLDMAN BAND CONCERT, CENTRAL PARK

came from Maine, Iowa, and Texas; from Australia, Yugoslavia, and China. On Central Park Mall, listening to Goldman's band, Georgia Negroes and French-Canadians jostled with Italians, Armenians, and Polish Jews. For a time after 1900 men were wont to say that Greater New York could be admired and could inspire loyalty, but could not be loved as a unit. A citizen might love Morningside or Columbia Heights or Staten Island, but hardly the whole of the fast-growing boroughs, the seven or eight million people, the complex of activities from the brokerage houses of Wall Street to the market gardens of Flushing, from the retail shops of Harlem to the factories on Newtown Creek.

[4]

LIBERTY BOND DRIVE, WORLD WAR I

Little by little, however, as the Greater City became more familiar to its residents, affection for all of it grew. Better communications gave the metropolis increasing unity. As immigration from abroad fell off, and as the schools did their work, its population struck down deeper roots and became more homogeneous. In time, when the Yankees led the League or the Dodgers ("dem bums") spurted forward, New Yorkers—whether of Manhattan or Kings or Queens, Staten Island, or the Bronx—thrilled as a unit. They felt a glow of common emotion when the hurdy-gurdy struck up "The Sidewalks of New York." They were enlivened as one great family when Mayor La Guardia lost his temper and exploded in a

[5]

NEW YORK WORLD'S FAIR, 1939

tantrum on the radio. They read O. Henry's stories as a reflection of the heart and mind of the town; stories the hero of which was the city itself, and which concentrated its essence so that "little old New York" really appeared small and homely, a true neighborhood. They invited country cousins and overseas uncles to the World's Fair, showing its sights with proprietary pride. Nor can the effect of the two global wars be forgotten. The parades on Fifth Avenue, the bond drives, the warm reception of Allied leaders, the exultant welcomes roared to Pershing in 1919 and Eisenhower in 1945 helped draw the city into a sense of comradeship.

[6]

As the Greater City thus slowly achieved unity, the citizenry nevertheless retained ample variety. Nobody ever believed that there was a New York type, a distinctive Gothamite as easily recognizable in alien zones as the London Cockney or Paris boulevardier. O. Henry had satirized the true New Yorker as a person who never looked west of the Hudson or south of the Bay:

"Been in the city long?" inquired the New Yorker, getting ready the exact tip against the waiter's coming with large change from the bill.

"Me?" said the man from Topaz City. "Four days. Never in Topaz City, was you?"

"I!" said the New Yorker. "I was never farther west than Eighth Avenue. I had a brother who died on Ninth, but I met the cortège at Eighth. There was a bunch of violets on the hearse, and the undertaker mentioned the incident to avoid mistake. I cannot say that I am familiar with the West."

That was a humorous bit of libel, for which O. Henry furnished amends in "The Making of a New Yorker" and in other tales. Plenty of New Yorkers came from Topaz City, Peoria, Tallahassee, Dallas, and other points from Maine to Catalina Island. Most of them are keenly interested in the rest of the country. In fact, the Greater New Yorker, like the American, is a medley of types and personalities. He is the apartment dweller whom Simeon Strunsky portrayed with kindly wit in his "Belshazzar Court" papers; he is the sociable, bustling, keen-witted Jewish citizen with whom Montague Glass dealt in his stories of Abe Potash and Mawruss Perlmutter, and Abraham Cahan in full-length novels; he is the lovable, irresponsible Irish householder of *A Tree Grows in Brooklyn;* he is the Wall Street clerk of Edwin Lefevre's stories of the financial district; he is the young newspaperman of Richard Harding

WAR NEWS FROM CHINA, CHINATOWN, 1938

Davis's pages; he is the brisk magazine editor of Howells's *Hazard of New Fortunes,* the district attorney of Arthur Train's fiction, the debutante of Edith Wharton's *House of Mirth,* the professional ballplayer of Ring Lardner, and the street gamin of E. W. Townsend's "Chimmie Fadden" books. Like the American in general, the citizen of Greater New York has tended to grow somewhat more uniform. School, radio, motion picture, newspaper, and office or factory have smoothed him toward a norm not at all unlike the citizen of Denver or Portland—but still he represents an infinite variety of origins and characteristics.

Perhaps the true New Yorker is simply the man, woman, or youth who loves the mighty ever-changing panorama of the metropolis, who responds to its surging vitality, and who

COACHING IN CENTRAL PARK, 1910   *Owned by The New-York Historical Society*

wants to see it freer of old bondages of vice and poverty, stronger intellectually and spiritually, and more hopeful in outlook. He is the man who thrills from old habit to those varied sights and sounds enumerated by Brander Matthews not long before the Greater City was born:

There was the Memorial Day parade; there was the private view of the National Academy of Design; there was the outpouring of families into lower Central Park on a Sunday afternoon in early spring; there was the annual Horse Show in Madison Square Garden in the late fall; and there was a roof-garden show on the top of some building in the middle of summer. There was Mulberry Bend in the swelter of a hot wave; and there was Wall Street blankly uninhabited on a holiday. There were the bobtailed cars, and the shrieking trains of the elevated railroad with

[9]

"SUICIDE CURVE," THE EL AT 110TH STREET

clouds of steam foaming down to become iridescent as the rays
of the setting sun shot through them. There was color everywhere, unending movement, incessant vitality.

He is the man who surrenders to the enchantment of Broadway on an early summer evening in the theatrical district—
the "Rialto" as Theodore Dreiser pictured it:

Here is the great city, and it is lush and dreamy. A May or June
moon will be hanging like a burnished silver disc between the
high walls aloft. A hundred, a thousand electric signs will wink
and blink, above the floods of citizens and visitors in summer
clothes and with gay hats; the street cars jouncing their endless
carloads on indifferent errands; the taxis and private cars flutter-
ing about like jeweled flies. The very gasoline contributes a distinct perfume. Life bubbles, sparkles; chatters gay, incoherent
stuff. Such is Broadway.

But he is also the man who remembers that New York is a
city of little people, of stenographers in Manhattan lodgings,
of small grocers on Brooklyn side streets, and of Tony the ice-
and-coal man in his Bronx basement. He remembers that the
test of the Greater City's success is its ability to improve their
lot, and that, to quote Simeon Strunsky, an anxious eye must
always be kept on its social standards:

A child growing up in New York probably has less chance of
being brought into contact with the criminal world than a child
growing up in Topeka, Kansas. . . . In recent years the murders
in New York have been four times the number of homicides in
Kansas, and the population of New York is four times that of
Kansas. New York, then, is not anti-social by the test of law and
order. It is not anti-social by the test of public health. The city's
death-rate is lower than that of Boston or Philadelphia or San
Francisco. It is a lower death-rate than in cities many times
smaller where one would expect less congestion and less stress
and strain—lower than Indianapolis or Hartford or Omaha. . . .

[11]

MACY'S THANKSGIVING DAY PARADE

Because the city has been remade in every generation, because so much of its population was born elsewhere, and because it lives so excitingly in the present, it has never shown the interest in municipal history which we find among Londoners and Parisians. Yet this history is so full of commanding figures, dramatic action, and contrasts of sunlight and shadow, that its principal scenes should be known to all citizens.

What we need is the imagination which would enable us to repeople old water fronts and streets with personages long dead. With that, how many scenes we might call up! Henry Hudson, perhaps, and his crew of rough Dutch and English seamen, leaning on the taffrail of the *Half Moon* as the ship creeps upstream with the tide past the marsh-fringed island of Manhattan, the men pointing eagerly as they glimpse a wolf slinking through the riverside thickets. Or, the grim fort at the Battery, with drums rattling, crowds staring, and clergymen praying as, in 1691, Jacob Leisler, leader of a popular uprising against the aristocratic families (the Bayards, Van Cortlandts, and others), spends his last moment on a gallows. Three high-spirited young men of the town, John Jay, Gouverneur Morris, and Robert R. Livingston, pacing up Broadway after a club gathering of "The Moot," and furiously discussing the latest article in Rivington's Tory newspaper as they go. The ragged, hungry mob roaring along Pearl Street in the bitter January weather of 1837, as panic and depression are strangling the country; angry placards swaying over their heads—"Bread! Meat! Rent! Prices Must Come Down!"—as they smash open warehouse doors and drag barrels and boxes of provisions out on the cobblestones. The grave, fashionable audience in the city's largest hall falling silent as one classic New Yorker, William Cullen Bryant, rises to deliver his memorial oration on another, Washington Irving. The dramatic moment when two processions, moving from each end of the newly completed Brooklyn Bridge, meet in the center, and two eminent public servants, Mayor Abram S. Hewitt of New York and Mayor Seth Low of Brooklyn, shake hands.

New Yorkers might find it easier to exercise this imaginative eye if more emphasis were laid on some of the parallels linking olden times with our later era. Those intellectual groups which are constantly complaining, with justice, that

STATEN ISLAND, 1897

they are badly rewarded, ought to know that this was always true, and that when the first schoolmaster of Manhattan failed to gain a fair living at his vocation, he made both ends meet by taking in washing. How many citizens of our time are aware that Mayor James J. Walker and the Royal Governor who presided over New York in the 1660s, that gallant cavalier Francis Lovelace, would have recognized each other as brothers?—for Lovelace had irresistible personal charm, loved gay amusements (he gave prizes for horse-racing on Long Island), organized a social club, gave little time to administrative cares, and had serious trouble with the Puritans. Have modern New Yorkers ever thought of the resemblances between the rum-runners of the recent Prohibition era and the old-time privateers (often verging on pirates), smugglers, and slavers who built snug fortunes out of the gains they brought into Manhattan? Do they know that Negroes were a much larger element of the city's population in colonial times than at any later period until the great flow into Harlem began?

Looking at the past, we can find a number of continuous strands that bind the little Anglo-Dutch seaport of the seven-

[14]

teenth and eighteenth centuries with the great world metropolis of today. One of these is the remarkable mixture of national stocks which has always distinguished New York above other cities of the globe, and the cosmopolitanism of mind and tolerance of spirit which have sprung therefrom. When Director Minuit held sway over the original village below Wall Street, it contained Dutch, English, Walloons, Huguenots, and Germans, not to speak of Negro and Indian slaves. These varied groups of Europeans intermarried freely. Religious barriers, except for brief periods, were slight. The same church building, in the days of Governor Thomas Dongan (himself an Irish gentleman of Roman Catholic faith) sheltered a Dutch Reformed congregation in the morning, Huguenots at noon, and Anglicans in the afternoon. The Jews planted a sturdy community in New York in 1654, twenty-three hardy pioneers arriving that year in the ship *St. Charles*. They conducted their own worship freely—and it was a Jew who lent money for building the first Lutheran church on the island. After 1820 began the tremendous modern immigration from abroad. "In no other city," wrote the novelist Anthony Trollope on his visit during the Civil War, "is there a population so mixed and cosmopolitan in their modes of life."

Misled by this heterogeneity, some critics used to call New York a foreign community; America, they suggested, began west of the Hudson. No slur could be further removed from the fact. Any visitor to New York might learn how deeply American the city is, Mr. Strunsky once remarked, by a short walking tour. He could begin at the Gramercy Park house of Samuel J. Tilden, a New Yorker through and through, who in 1876 received a majority of the popular vote for President. He could then stroll westward to the house on

[15]

East Twentieth which stands as a replica of the birthplace of Theodore Roosevelt, with the furniture which T.R. knew as a boy and youth. From that point the tourist could walk uptown, passing the place where Chester A. Arthur long lived in the old Eighteenth Assembly District, to 816 Madison Avenue. Here, in the days before an apartment house replaced it, stood a solid, upright Victorian house in which dwelt that solid upright Victorian statesman, Grover Cleveland. From that point it is but a short distance to the town house of Franklin D. Roosevelt on East Sixty-fifth Street; and from there in turn it is not far to the apartment house on Fifth Avenue, overlooking the picturesque arsenal in Central Park, where Alfred E. Smith was long to be found. Where is

Brown Brothers

V-E DAY, 1945

another American city with a roster of national leaders like this?—and a group more authentically American?

Another of the great strands tying together all eras of the city, past and present, is trade. Upon commerce its greatness was first built, and upon commerce it continues to rest. In the earliest years fisheries and whaling were important; whales were killed even inside the Lower Bay. The colonial wars with France and Spain made privateering a source of wealth. Long before the Revolution, New York ships were known everywhere. They ranged the coast from the Penobscot to the St. John. They traded with the West Indies and Africa, and with bustling ports of Britain and the Spanish Main. New York tills were full not of guineas alone, but of moidores, pistoles, livres, kroner and Spanish dollars. Taverns along the water front were crowded with rough fellows in pigtails, larding their talk with foreign phrases, and dangerous with Swedish or Italian steel. After the Revolution, trade with India and China grew brisk. New York shops displayed Oriental shawls, spices, perfumes, rugs, and jewels alongside the silks and wines of the Mediterranean, and the china, furniture, textiles, and ironware of Britain and France.

Then enterprising citizens nailed into place, one after another, the three great rungs on the ladder by which nineteenth century New York climbed to a decisive leadership among American cities. The building of the Erie Canal, after plans first made by Gouverneur Morris and others, but boldly executed by De Witt Clinton, threw open the whole West to the city. Originally its hinterland had been confined to the valleys of the Hudson, Connecticut, and Raritan. But when the canal was completed in 1825, all the wide basin of the Great Lakes was made tributary to New York merchants, middlemen, and bankers. Before many years passed, Father

SHIPPING IN THE NINETIES   *Brown Brothers*

Knickerbocker was handling two-thirds of the country's imports, while he drew to his portals an increasing share of the exports. In 1820, for example, Baltimore had supplied the principal channel by which American flour went to Europe; by 1830 New York was easily the nation's chief flour-shipper. The second rung of the ladder was the creation of the "cotton triangle." New York merchants sent packets to Charles-

TWENTIETH CENTURY TRAVEL

ton, Mobile, or New Orleans, laden with general merchandise; carried cotton from these ports to England and France; and fetched back to New York immigrants and general freight. Thus they forestalled the rise of a direct trade from Southern ports and reaped a full share of profit from cotton production. Nor was the city behind in railway construction, its third rung in the climb toward primacy. Constructing

BROOKLYN BRIDGE   *Brown Brothers*

first the Erie and then the Hudson River-New York Central railroads to the Great Lakes, it kept the well-established Western trading connections in its own hands, safe from undue encroachments by jealous mercantile houses of Boston, Philadelphia, and Baltimore.

When Lincoln was elected President, nearly 70 percent of the nation's imports flowed in through New York, and about one-third of its exports poured out by the city. What the metropolis had thus gained it has continued to hold. In time it eclipsed Liverpool and London. The close of World War I found it not only the first American port, but the foremost among the world's ports.

Another continuing strand in city history is not merely conspicuous but particularly pleasing. Because of its cosmopolitan population, primacy in trade, and position as the chief port of entry for immigrants, New York has always stood foremost in the transmission of cultural forces between the Old World and the New. It has been the principal disseminator of European ideas. Other cities, like Boston, may have produced as much in pure literature; others, like Chicago, may have been as restlessly creative in art and architecture. But New York, from the days of Alexander Hamilton's studenthood, Tom Paine's residence, and Carl Schurz's entry, down to the present-day "University in Exile," has done by far the most to shelter foreign refugees. New York, from the time of John La Farge's birth in 1835 among the Gallic families which had escaped the French or Dominican revolutions, and from Augustus St. Gaudens's childhood, has done the most to introduce European ideas of art. From its opera houses and concert halls (the halls of Maretzek, Augustus Thomas, and Leopold Damrosch, not to mention later figures), foreign music has spread throughout the nation. New York has always had its foreign-language newspapers of distinction—the *Staats-Zeitung* and *Courrier des Etats-Unis* are well over a century old; it has had a long series of British-born editors, from William Cobbett and James Gordon Bennett to Edwin L. Godkin. It has always been the capital of the Anglo-American stage in this country; the stage of Kean, Macready, the Booths, Sothern, and the "royal family" of the Drews and the Barrymores. From Duncan Phyfe, the Scot, bringing to his shop on Fulton Street the beautiful furniture designs which still influence American craftsmen, to the Yugoslav dancer Tashamira bringing interpretations which affect choreography all over the country, New York has been incessantly active as a mediator of culture.

We might speak of other continuing traditions in the city's history. One is the tradition of gaiety: the attention to recreation, showmanship, gastronomic delights, and social life, which perhaps reached its height in the so-called Night Club

5TH AVENUE AT THE TURN OF THE CENTURY   *Brown Brothers*

Era. Even Henry James, in his book on America, spoke of the city as "so nocturnal, so bacchanal, so hugely hatted and feathered and flounced." Other cities, however, are also gay. It would be safer to note as a dominant strand since colonial times the city's leadership in fashion. From the stately early period of the DeLanceys, Crugers, De Peysters, and Bayards through the rococo years of Ward McAllister's Four Hundred, the city always had a special *ton*. If fashions were not made in Pearl Street and on Fifth Avenue, they were confirmed there. Miss Flora McFlimsey of Madison Square, who spent weeks in shopping at home and abroad, only to lament that she had "nothing to wear," helped build up a cult of the costume. From the balls and routs of the colonial governors to the James Hazen Hyde affair which transformed Sherry's into a replica of the court of Louis XIV, entertainment in

[22]

New York set the American pace. The great American merchant, long before John Wanamaker or Marshall Field were dreamed of, was A. T. Stewart of New York; Tiffany's was the country's most fashionable jeweler; Goupil's and the Dusseldorf Gallery placed a special seal of distinction upon paintings. Ideas of modishness have changed, and the old-time aristocracy is no more. Yet, since the impoverishment of European centers, New York holds a greater place in making fashions than ever.

It is with the history of the first fifty years of Greater New York, however, that we are specially concerned. In no period has the city made history on ampler lines, or of a more creditable kind. In glancing at this half-century, we can but point out a few of the most significant changes; changes so remarkable that they may almost be termed revolutionary.

One especially momentous transformation must be noted at the outset. The city's growth, unceasing and sometimes titanic, has for the first time been controlled by plan. On May 7, 1912, civic organizations and prominent citizens met in a City Plan Conference. The result of this and certain allied efforts was the writing of two epochal amendments to the City Charter. One gave the Board of Estimate power to district the city according to the use made of property, confining the area of different industries and trades. The other permitted the Board to divide the city into sections wherein buildings should conform to fixed requirements as to height and percentage of ground covered. The zoning legislation of 1916 followed. All this made it possible to restrict the garment trades, for example, whose uptown march had threatened the shopping and theatrical districts, to a special area. It made possible the preservation of the amenities of upper Fifth Avenue, from the beautiful Public Library, which had been begun in 1902, to the Carnegie and Phipps mansions constructed at 90th and 87th Streets soon afterward. High buildings would have ruined the Avenue; the zoning legislation restricted height to 150 feet. The Fifth Avenue Association, organized in 1907 to safeguard the famous thoroughfare, is but one of numerous organizations designed to protect and further city planning.

Following the zoning legislation, one great step after another was taken in planning. The Port of New York Authority was established in 1921 to design communications and port facilities for the whole district. The Regional Plan Association was organized in 1929. The Municipal Housing Authority was created in 1934. The decade of the 1920s was specially notable for the work of the planning committee brought together with Charles D. Norton as chairman and Daniel Burnham's Chicago Plan as its chief inspiration. The studies of this committee carried home to all who read them the criminal waste of unplanned community development. As Mr. Norton pointed out, hundreds of millions of public money had been thrown away on piecemeal, unrelated, ill-considered building; the private losses were far greater still. Boldly grasping its opportunity, the Regional Plan Committee determined to survey the entire region within a fifty-mile circle drawn from City Hall; a region stretching from Princeton to Newburgh, and from the Morristown hills in Jersey to the Westchester ridges, to Bridgeport, and to the tip of Long Island. On Norton's death in 1923 his place was taken by Frederic A. Delano. They and their chief associates in bringing out the ten volumes of the Regional Survey—Thomas Adams, Cass Gilbert, Henry James, W. J. Wilgus, Harvey W. Corbett, F. L. Olmsted, Lawson Purdy, George McAneny—deserve a high rank among the city's benefactors.

THE OLD RESERVOIR, 5TH AVENUE AT 42D STREET

THE NEW YORK PUBLIC LIBRARY

[25]

Already the planning has borne magnificent fruit. From it have sprung express highways ribboning the East River and the Hudson; the Henry Hudson Parkway; the cloverleaf of the Triborough Bridge; the Interborough Parkway from Kew Gardens to Brooklyn; and the bridge across Rockaway Inlet. The plan has given Robert Moses a better basis for his memorable work as Park Commissioner; a work which has developed for the city, among other amenities, the Jacob Riis and Juniper Valley parks in Queens, Red Hook Park in Brooklyn, and the recreational grounds on Ward and Randall islands. Meanwhile, the activities of the Port Authority have endowed Greater New York, alongside more prosaic works, with the Lincoln and Holland Tunnels, the George Washington, Goethals, and Bayonne Bridges, and the Outerbridge Crossing. Mayors La Guardia and O'Dwyer consistently lent effective aid to the city planners, and so have certain Federal agencies. The idea that Greater New York and its environs can be patterned to a far happier model had been completely vindicated by 1948.

Second among the revolutionary developments of the half-century unquestionably stands the efflorescence of agencies for the higher expression of culture. When the Greater City was formed, no impartial critic would have placed New York on a parity with London, Paris, or Berlin as a cultural center. Its universities, libraries, museums, and research institutions were both weaker and more elementary. Fifty years later, despite gaps still to be filled, the city stands preeminent in its cultural facilities. Bare mention can be given to a few of the steps by which it reached this height, for a full history would fill volumes.

The removal of Columbia to Morningside Heights at almost the same time as the establishment of the Greater

STATESMAN VIVIANI AND MARSHAL JOFFRE
RECEIVE THE LL.D. AT COLUMBIA

City, the flood of gifts to it in the first decade of the century, the enterprising policies of President Butler, and the appointment of a remarkable corps of teachers, lifted that institution from its old semi-collegiate status to the rank of a powerful university. Teachers College became part of Co-

[27]

lumbia's educational system in 1898; the graduate School of Journalism, founded by Joseph Pulitzer, was added in 1912; the School of Business was organized in 1916; and a new era in the history of the medical branch began when in 1921 the College of Physicians and Surgeons was affiliated with Presbyterian Hospital for the establishment of the vigorous uptown Medical Center. Much could be said of the parallel expansion of New York University, which entered its uptown quarters on University Heights in 1895, and which, with teachers busy there, in the original home on Washington Square, in the Bronx, and at Hempstead, now ministers to some forty thousand students. Much could be said of City College, which dedicated its Gothic stone buildings (using Manhattan schist) on St. Nicholas Heights in 1908, and which found a specially gifted leader in John H. Finley. The city which had no university of the first rank in 1898 possessed three fifty years later. Indeed, since the rapid development of Fordham University, the largest Catholic seat of higher learning in the country, it may well lay claim to four.

Again, when the Greater City was created, it had no library of the highest distinction. How could it? The consolidation of the Astor and Lenox Libraries and the Tilden Trust had just been effected (1895), ending an unfortunate division of resources. These combined libraries had no adequate home. But with generous city aid, and the wise, practical, and somewhat dictatorial John Shaw Billings to draft plans, rapid advances were made. Billings reclassified the collections, built up the holdings, persuaded Carnegie to give five million dollars for branches, and lent vigor to every activity. When Carrère and Hastings finished their neoclassic structure of white Vermont marble in 1911, space temporarily seemed abundant. There was room for the splendid basic

[28]

collections in science, history, economics, music, and other departments, for the fifty thousand rare books, for the growing manuscript collections, and for such special gifts as the Jacob Schiff library of Jewish materials. Billings had able successors. By 1948 the four and a quarter million volumes of the library, the second in the Western Hemisphere and the third or fourth in the world, overcrowded its quarters, and it was still growing fast. It was one of the principal fortresses of learning and research in the land.

The banner was similarly carried forward by other institutions. While New York in 1898 had good music schools, none ranked with the best of Europe; but in 1920 the will of Augustus D. Juilliard created a foundation on which a distinguished institution could be reared. The Greater City at first contained no well-staffed center for medical inquiry. Then the Rockefeller Institute for Medical Research, established in 1901 with a corps of scientists headed by Simon Flexner, soon rose to a fame surpassed by none in the world. Professional organizations, as the years passed, concentrated large resources for research in New York. The library of the Bar Association, with more than two hundred thousand volumes, is perhaps excelled only by the legal collections of the Library of Congress; an admirable technological collection is housed in the building of the Engineering Societies; a huge medical library in that of the Academy of Medicine. The Morgan Library of rare books and manuscripts, occupying a building erected in 1913 and an annex added fifteen years later, is renowned among scholars of literature.

Indeed, almost every field of culture is represented in the city's panoply, and in most of them facilities for the highest type of study have been created. There are well-equipped libraries of art and illustrative material at the Metropolitan

Museum, the Frick Gallery, and the Cooper Union. The Natural History Museum offers many aids to advanced work. In 1903 George C. Heye established his Museum of the American Indian, whose steadily growing collections are indispensable to students of ethnology, archaeology, and anthropology. The generosity of Archer M. Huntington housed it in one of the units of his uptown cultural center (many people think, too far uptown, but time may change that), including Huntington's own Hispanic Museum, the Numismatic Museum, and the home of the American Geographical Society. In this group of buildings, erected on land which formerly was part of the old J. J. Audubon estate, stand also the quarters of the National Institute and American Academy of Art and Letters, with their picked intellectual membership.

Another of the sweeping changes of the half-century lies in the greatly enhanced part played by women in the city's life. When Greater New York was formed, no woman voted, none held office, and, while some were distinguished in the professions, few occupied places of power in business. To be sure, early in the new century a few achieved prominence in social work. They included Maud Nathan, who with Josephine Lowell had founded the Consumers' League; Florence Kelly, secretary of that organization; Lillian Wald, head of the Henry Street Nurses' Settlement; Maud Ballington Booth of the Volunteers of America; and Dr. Annie Daniels, a leader in public health. But women were determined not to be kept in a constricted field. With a growing confidence in their equal capacity with men, they earned places of high responsibility.

Not least in public affairs. The Mitchel Administration appointed the first woman as head of a city department:

RED CROSS PARADE, 1918

Brown Brothers

Katharine Bement· Davis, long in charge of the State Re-
formatory for Women, was named Commissioner of Correc-
tion. Soon after suffrage was introduced, some of the ablest
members of the state and county committees of both parties
were women. Mary Simkhovitch, for decades head of Greenwich House (one of the country's most noted settlements),
became the chief adviser of Alfred E. Smith on social and
economic problems. Another New York social worker, Frances Perkins, after directing the State Factory Commission
Inquiry inspired by the Triangle fire, and serving as chairman of the State Industrial Board, was made Secretary of
Labor—the first woman in the Cabinet. Still another New
Yorker, Eleanor Roosevelt, had a position of influence in her
own right as vice-principal of the Todhunter School, vice-

[31]

president of the League of Women Voters, and active social reformer, before her husband became President. The fiftieth anniversary of the Greater City found women well established on the bench: Anna M. Kross and Frances Lehrich were city magistrates, and Justine Wise Polier and Jane A. Bolin were justices of the Domestic Relations Court.

Women's organizations and women's share in general organizations had both expanded. An early defeat for a suffrage amendment to the state constitution had led six women, including Catherine A. B. Abbe, founder of the City History Club, and Dr. Mary Putnam Jacobi, first woman member of the New York Academy of Medicine, to take steps for the establishment of Town Hall. This was just beginning a full program of work under Robert E. Ely when the Greater City was formed; and another woman, Anna B. Bliss, launched the movement which resulted in the present Town Hall building and the forming of Town Hall Club. Women were always active in the Foreign Policy Association, and by 1948 Vera Michaeles Dean was the chief figure in that body. The Women's City Club and the League of Women Voters have both done sterling service for political education and the furtherance of sound public policies; while the Cosmopolitan Club and Colony Club have lent their aid to many a good cause.

The high place of women among journalists and authors is of course an old story. They had produced capable editorial workers, such as Margaret Fuller, Kate Field, and Ida M. Tarbell, long before the rise of such widely read writers of our own time as Dorothy Thompson and Anne O'Hare McCormick. There had been precursors of Mrs. Wharton and Miss Cather—though none who approached their eminence. But it remained for the first half-century of the

Greater City to produce women who would largely direct the destinies of great metropolitan dailies, like Helen Reid of the *Herald-Tribune* and Dorothy Schiff Thackrey of the New York *Post*. Not before this period did a woman edit an influential political weekly, as Freda Kirchwey has edited the *Nation*. No woman had ever occupied quite such a place in the business world as that held by Dorothy Shaver, head of Lord & Taylor. A number of women lawyers, among whom it is hardly invidious to name Dorothy Straus, have won high place at the bar, and in the course of their hard fight they gained admittance to the Bar Association. Great as was the place which in 1898 Charlotte Perkins Gilman and Carrie Chapman Catt desired for women, by 1948 it had been fairly well occupied in New York.

One other revolutionary change remains to be noted: the enormously enhanced attention, both private and public, to social welfare measures. Fifty years ago the allotments in the municipal budget for health, housing, and relief were slender. New York as much as London had its "submerged tenth"; Jacob Riis had found, indeed, that about 10 percent of the city's population could not pay for a decent grave and so were buried in Potter's Field. The unemployed, the ailing, the defective, and the underprivileged had to beg for charity. Today the emphasis falls not upon philanthropy, but social justice. The prime object of the city is not the mere alleviation of misery, but its prevention. Men and women are to be better housed; children are to be better fed and schooled; immigrants are to be better guided; the ill are to be helped early by clinics and hospitals; Negroes and the populous new Puerto Rican community are to be lifted to opportunity. Crime is to be prevented by more parks, more playgrounds, more schooling, and by the crime-prevention branch of the

[33]

Police Department; while delinquent boys are to be aided in the Adolescents' Court and erring girls in the Wayward Minors Court.

In all of its boroughs, the city's park area was more than doubled during the 1930s. Play streets and playgrounds are now accepted as a prime responsibility of the municipal authorities. Particularly in housing, a wholly new attitude, which such pioneers as Alfred T. White and Richard Watson Gilder would have found inspiring, has appeared. When the City Housing Authority was set up in 1934, with Langdon W. Post as chairman, it found slum conditions truly appalling. In the "blighted districts" of the Greater City a half-million families or more were, in its words, "condemned to live lives of squalor and degradation." The Authority mapped out a broad program for the demolition of slum

Wide World

BOATING IN CENTRAL PARK

WILLIAMSBURG PLAYGROUND

New York City Department of Parks

property and the construction of excellent low-rent housing; and as models for future work it collaborated with the PWA in erecting the Harlem River Houses in upper Manhattan and the Ten Eyck Houses in the Williamsburg section of Brooklyn. Since then the city, the Federal Government, such philanthropic citizens as John D. Rockefeller, Jr., and several of the wealthiest insurance companies have labored together in the rehabilitation of slum neighborhoods. It is a tremendous task—the rebuilding of the lower East Side of Manhattan alone would cost at least half a billion—but more than a beginning has been made.

Altogether, an entirely new social outlook has appeared since 1898: an outlook in which government is seen as responsible for the welfare of the whole population, lines of class and nationality have been partly broken down by a more fraternal democracy, and equity has replaced charity as a principle of action. The city has its terrible dark areas. The contrast between wealth and abject poverty in blocks not half a mile apart is still glaring. Difficult problems are bound up in the gravitation of depressed groups to the metropolis, for under political pressures paternalism can be carried too far. To meet the task, the city has mobilized its energies far more effectively than ever before. It has about twelve hundred social agencies of all types, of which nearly five hundred operate in the field of family relief and services, and nearly a hundred in maternity work. It has more than fifteen hundred clinics. Municipal and private activities have been increasingly coordinated. Under Mayors La Guardia and O'Dwyer no backward step has been permitted in health, housing, or home relief (for which, alone, more than $160,-000,000 has been provided in the 1948 budget).

It would be easy to speak of still other changes. Much could be said of the movements and displacements of population, the shifting position of Irish-Americans, Jewish-Americans, Italian-Americans, and others during the half-century. These changes have helped fill the once-empty spaces of Richmond, Queens, and the Bronx. Much could be said of the marked—if jerky and uneven—forward movement in city government. When the Greater City was formed the ugly revelations of the Lexow Investigation were a recent memory. It is a far cry from Gilroy and Croker in the 1890s to La Guardia and O'Dwyer in the 1940s, from the old corrupt Board of Aldermen to the more efficient and civic-minded (if

ASTORIA PARK, QUEENS

New York City Department of Parks
Wide World

BOTANIC GARDENS, PROSPECT PARK, BROOKLYN

[37]

not absolutely perfect) City Council of today. These, however, are changes which New York has shared with other American communities, from Boston to Los Angeles. All over the country, the long battle for greater municipal efficiency began to gain substantial victories after 1900.

What of the future? City life is the hope of the modern world. All the progressive nations, including America, have become highly urbanized; and in all of them the city provides the fullest opportunity for intellectual growth, individual enterprise, and cultural achievement. As the richest, strongest, and largest of the world's cities, New York stands in a long historic line: Memphis, Babylon, Athens, Rome, Florence, Paris, London, all had their day of supremacy—and now the torch has passed to our own municipality. Will it be worthy of its position?

Its people must give the answer. Greatness is not conferred by magnitude and money, by cloud-capped towers and gorgeous palaces, by pomp and power. These may be means to greatness or impediments, according to the spiritual quality of the men and women who use them. Greatness is never material; it is moral, intellectual, and spiritual. As New Yorkers, celebrating the fiftieth year of the Greater City, peer down the long vista of years ahead, they may well think of certain spiritual symbols in their midst. One is the statue of Liberty Enlightening the World, with her torch held aloft for the ships and peoples of all nations entering the harbor to see. One is the Brooklyn Bridge, together with the other bridges that link the boroughs and bind New York with the Jersey mainland, a symbol of the fact that cities and nations no longer wall themselves in, but thrust forth lines of communication for mutual comradeship and assistance. One, the grandest of all, is the capitol building of the

[38]

United Nations, hope and augury of a bright new day of international association and world solidarity. The eight million people who dwell in the shadow of these mighty symbols have no excuse if they fail to rise to their unprecedented opportunities.

THE STATUE OF LIBERTY

CITY HALL, 1853

Wide World
Museum of the City of New York

THE BATTERY, 1898

Framing the Charter

By JOHN A. KROUT

"THE SUN will rise this morning upon the greatest experiment in municipal government that the world has ever known—the enlarged city. . . . The end of the old New York and the beginning of the greater city were marked last night by perhaps the biggest, noisiest and most hilarious New Year's Eve celebration that Manhattan Island has ever known." Thus did the New York *Tribune* on January 1, 1898, hail the creation of the new metropolis.

The public demonstration in the closing hours of the old year had reached its climax at City Hall. There Hearst's alert associates on the New York *Journal* had appropriately arranged everything for the formal ceremonies, except the weather. A cold rain fell early in the evening, turning to damp snow before midnight. But the big eyes of many a searchlight winked intermittent flashes of daylight over City Hall Park and the surrounding streets. Red and green flares and set pieces of fireworks of every description sent rainbow effects high into the foggy air. Aerial bombs exploded; and a huge balloon trailing skirts of colored flame floated out toward the harbor. By the time the procession of prominent citizens, civic organizations, and singing societies, with a long line of brilliantly illuminated floats, reached the scene, the police were having difficulty maintaining their lines

CITY HALL, 1937

against the throngs along the west side of Broadway and the east side of Park Row. The hundreds of voices in the combined choral societies could scarcely be heard above the shrieking whistles of the tugs and ferry boats in the rivers.

As the hands of the clock moved toward twelve, there was a solemn moment. Mayor Phelan of San Francisco, in his office far across the continent, touched an electric button and the city ensign of Greater New York rose slowly to the top of the flagstaff on City Hall. The chimes of Trinity Church "rang out the old," and the multitude, led by the German singing societies, lifted its voice in "Auld Lang Syne" before the music was overwhelmed in the raucous noise of jubilation.

The reporter who remarked that the flag of Greater New York rose rather unsteadily to the top of the flagstaff may have been thinking about the uncertainties, the difficulties, the bitterness which had marked the struggle to achieve political consolidation. The controversy had been drawn out over many years; and some who had finally supported the idea of union had done so reluctantly, unconvinced that it would solve the problems of municipal government which, as James Bryce had forcefully pointed out, were usually so ineptly handled in America.

It is impossible to determine the origin of the idea that the boundaries of the City of New York should be expanded to include Brooklyn, Long Island City, Staten Island, and the surrounding towns and villages. Brooklynites thought

Wide World

BROOKLYN BOROUGH HALL

BOROUGH HALL, QUEENS

BOROUGH HALL, RICHMOND

that they had detected Manhattan's expansionist tendencies as early as 1833, when their petition to the state legislature for a municipal charter had been opposed by the Mayor and aldermen of New York on the ground that incorporation of Brooklyn should occur only in connection with New York. After Brooklyn became a city in 1834, little talk of union was heard for twenty years; but by mid-century the developing commerce of the busy harbor created difficulties which could not be quickly resolved by separate political entities. In 1857 Henry C. Murphy, a former Mayor of Brooklyn, who was to be President Buchanan's Minister to the Netherlands, spoke for many discerning businessmen when he said: "It requires no spirit of prophecy to foretell the union of New York and Brooklyn at no distant day. The river which divides them will soon cease to be a line of separation, and, bestrode by the colossus of commerce, will prove a link which will bind them together." In 1874, New York annexed three townships—Kingsbridge, West Farms, and Morrisania —lying west of the Bronx River in Westchester County.

For more than forty years, however, Greater New York was but an idea in men's minds. That it finally became reality was primarily the result of the intelligent and persistent activity of one man—Andrew Haswell Green. His was that unselfish devotion to high ideals which has ever marked the true reformer. While a member of the New York Park Board in 1868, he became convinced that any system of public improvements, to be successful, would have to be supported by the whole metropolitan district. That, he insisted, meant the political integration of the territory surrounding the City of New York into a great municipality. So steadfastly did he present his arguments that the plan for consolidation became known as "Green's hobby"; but the single-

BRONX COUNTY BUILDING

ness of purpose which the term implied was not marred by any hint of folly.

Although Andrew H. Green liked to point out that the lines of unity had been laid down by nature when it "grouped together in close indissoluble relation, at the mouth of a great river, our three islands, Manhattan, Long and Staten, making them buttresses and breakwaters of a capacious harbor," he was quite unwilling to wait patiently for nature to take its course. During the seventies and eighties he had strong support in the New York press, and a Municipal Union Society listed the advantages—lower taxes,

[46]

increased realty values, better municipal services—which would result from the creation of a Greater New York. The legislators at Albany received numerous petitions and gave serious consideration to several bills which would have brought Brooklyn and New York under a common government.

Such opposition as the friends of consolidation encountered came in large measure from Brooklyn. If the construction of the East River Bridge and its opening in 1883 gave new impetus to the demands of New Yorkers for territorial expansion, it produced the opposite effect on Long Island. Brooklyn's leading newspapers, the *Eagle* and the *Standard-Union,* may not have spoken for the majority of their readers, but they were forthright in opposing annexation to New York. "We might have thought of matrimony once," said the *Eagle,* "but now it is out of the question." To this the *Standard-Union* added: "What New York would do for or with Brooklyn if it had the power can be imagined, and the people of the latter, without regard to party, do not intend to try the experiment. They will hold on to their independence and take care of themselves."

Green and his associates realized that this sentiment could not be dismissed as unreasonable provincialism, and they redoubled their efforts to persuade their reluctant fellow citizens. With some help from the state administration, under Governor David B. Hill, they secured the passage of an act, which the Governor approved on May 8, 1890, creating "a commission to inquire into the expediency of consolidating the various municipalities in the State of New York occupying the several islands in the harbor of New York." No powerful opponents of consolidation were named to the Board; and, with Andrew Green in the chair and J. S.

T. Stranahan, a prominent Brooklyn advocate of union as the vice-president, it was not difficult to guess what the final report would be. The commissioners, having heard testimony on both sides, drafted a bill advocating immediate creation of a Greater New York.

The legislature, however, moved with caution. It took almost four years to devise a formula which suited the majority. Then, in 1894, the consolidationists won their first major victory. A bill was passed enabling the voters in the metropolitan district to vote on the question of consolidation. There were rumors of a "deal" between Democratic and Republican politicians; but it is more likely that the lobby in favor of the bill had finally convinced the influential leaders at Albany that a popular referendum on the subject was politically harmless. However that may be, the proponents of a greater city were ready to seize their opportunity. Arguments often heard in committee room and private conference were now restated to make a wider public appeal. The informal groups which had been working earnestly through the years now sought more effective organization.

By common consent Brooklyn was considered the chief battleground. There, more than on Manhattan Island, the roots of local loyalty had struck deeply, giving strength to those who wanted to preserve the social characteristics of an earlier day. Brooklynites who cherished the image of their city as a small community of homes, schools and churches, little touched by the urgencies of manufacturing and commerce, were unpersuaded when they heard that metropolitan consolidation would mean more population, greater business opportunities, lower taxes, lower interest on mortgages, increased employment and more extensive public works. They

BATTERY PLACE AND BOWLING GREEN, 1898 *Museum of the City of New York*

doubted that the problems of their own municipal government, which were too often mishandled by the political machine, could be solved by adding the problems of another municipality, which had experienced similar difficulties under an even more powerful political machine.

Fortunately for the expansionists, they had the aid of the Consolidation League, an organization which claimed more than 40,000 enrolled voters in 1894. It served in the campaign as a spearhead for the friends of a Greater New York, mobilizing civic reformers, politicians, businessmen, real estate speculators, in a supreme effort to win the plebiscite. In the end superior organization won—a narrow victory. Brooklyn cast 64,744 votes in favor of consolidation and 64,-467 against. In other parts of the metropolitan district the results were more decisive. New York, Queens, and Richmond counties rolled up a favorable majority of almost 44,-000 votes; while the little towns of Eastchester and Pelham gave 625 in favor and 413 against. The final tabulation for the metropolitan district showed that consolidation had been favored by 176,170 and rejected by 131,706.

Andrew Green and his enthusiastic colleagues interpreted this vote as a mandate to proceed at once with consolidation. During the weeks following the election they made sure that they had the support of the incoming administration of Governor Levi P. Morton. In his first message to the legislators in January, 1895, Governor Morton proposed that "a commission be at once created to be composed of the most capable citizens of the various localities interested, and to be charged with the power and the duty of framing a charter and reporting the same to the present legislature."

While the legislature debated the proper terms of such a bill, popular sentiment against consolidation seemed to be rising. In New York the election of Mayor William L. Strong on a reform platform had weakened the support of certain Democratic politicians who had been favorable; in Brooklyn the closeness of the vote in the recent referendum had encouraged the opponents of consolidation. The more determined among them formed the League of Loyal Citizens under the leadership of William C. Redfield, who was

BUSINESSMEN'S PARADE, 1896

Brown Brothers

later to become Secretary of Commerce in the cabinet of
Woodrow Wilson. They soon claimed an active membership of 50,000; established an efficient legislative lobby in
Albany; and financed a vigorous publicity campaign to prevent the passage of any consolidation bill.

To Green and Stranahan and their associates, the League
and its followers were standing in the way of progress. By

refusing to accept the trend of events, they were playing into the hands of professional politicians who hated to lose their power. Loyalty to an independent Brooklyn was curtly dismissed as "a sort of senile sentimentalism that is really quite incapable of appreciating the changes that the lapse of time demands for the development of great thriving communities, and which vainly strives to stay the wheels of beneficient progress."

The influence of the League, however, could not be ignored. It reached as far as Albany, where it was strengthened by the support of residents of New York who had begun to doubt whether such municipal problems as taxation, transportation, fire and police protection, public health and sanitation, parks and public improvements would be brought any nearer solution by extending the boundaries of their city. No one can say how important this opposition was in determining the vote of the legislators. At any rate, when a bill to permit consolidation and to authorize the preparation of a charter for the proposed Greater New York came before the Senate, it was defeated by two votes, with every Senator from Brooklyn and New York City voting in the negative.

Thus, the legislative session of 1895 ended in disappointment for the consolidationists. They had to be content with the passage of an act, known as the Annexation Bill, which permitted New York to acquire certain additional territory in Westchester County east of the Bronx River—Throg's Neck, Unionport, Westchester, Williamsbridge, Bronxdale, Olinville, Baychester, Eastchester, Wakefield, Bartow—bringing the city line north to Yonkers, Mount Vernon, Pelham, and New Rochelle. Behind the scenes, however, they were winning influential supporters, none more important than Thomas C. Platt, "boss" of the state Republican organiza-

[52]

tion. For many years Platt had been either opposed or indifferent to consolidation, but by the autumn of 1895 he was ready to give the proposal his political blessing. The reasons for his change in attitude are not entirely clear. Probably his friends were too kind when they attributed his new position to that "patriotic and constructive statesmanship" which realized that "consolidation was right and logical and necessary to the complete and rational development of the metropolis." He may have realized also that the charter of Greater New York could be framed along lines reviving the legislative commission system, with the probability of Republican stalwarts securing the controlling positions.

When Governor Morton reminded the legislature in 1896 that he still desired a law for the consolidation of the metropolitan area, his words seemed to be in the form of a command. Every legislator knew that "Boss" Platt was now openly supporting the proposal, and many had heard rumors of a "deal" between the Republican state organization and the leaders of Tammany Hall. A law was quickly passed authorizing a joint committee of assemblymen and senators to investigate the desirability of extending the boundaries of New York. With Senator Clarence Lexow as chairman, the committee listened to petitions and counter-petitions revealing the division of sentiment in both New York and Brooklyn; and then asked the legislature to create a charter commission and set January 1, 1898, as the date for the establishment of Greater New York.

While this recommendation was making its way—and a stormy way it was—through the State Assembly, the friends and foes of consolidation had renewed their warfare. The lines of division were not hard and fast, for men changed their minds on the subject as they tried to calculate all of its implications. For example, Seth Low, president of Columbia University and long a consolidationist, now joined with former Mayor Abram S. Hewitt, Elihu Root, and other members of the City Club in a petition to the legislature, protesting that the Lexow Bill would force New York to annex territory "that has either been deprived for a long time of local improvements, or has been driven by the peculiarity of its position into a recklessness born of indifference." The *Tribune* warned its readers that consolidation should not be adopted until the details had been carefully worked out and critically examined.

Citizens of New York, who joined the Taxpayers Anti-Equalization League, fearing an increase in their tax bills, were encouraged by the determined resistance to annexation in Brooklyn. President Redfield of the League of Loyal Citizens guided the propaganda and tactics of his organization so adroitly that its members seemed to represent the dominant opinion in their city. They secured more than seventy thousand signatures to a petition requesting the Legislature to resubmit the question to the voters. Theodore B. Willis, leader of the local Republican machine, and Dr. Littlejohn, Episcopal Bishop of Long Island, agreed that Brooklyn had a spirit and tradition of its own which would be destroyed by union with New York.

On the other side, there were also strong forces. The combativeness of Dana's *Sun* and the editorial vigor of Pulitzer's *World* steadily sustained the expansionists. In Brooklyn they had to be content with the support of the *Citizen*, but it was widely read by organization Democrats and by persons active in labor circles. Among businessmen, Stranahan and his associates in the Consolidation League were still influential, and they had now the cooperation of such civic leaders as Lewis

THE BLIZZARD OF '99

THE BLIZZARD OF '47

[55]

M. Peck and William J. Gaynor, who was later to become Mayor of Greater New York.

The decisive factor in the situation was the power of Tom Platt. Without his aid the Lexow Bill would not have passed the Assembly. Even with his unfailing support the bill barely received the necessary votes. When his own lieutenants failed him, Platt turned to Tammany and found there his margin of victory.

Under the State Constitution, as revised in 1894, the mayors of the cities affected by the Lexow Bill had the right to accept or reject it. Since both Mayor Frederick Wurster of Brooklyn and Mayor William L. Strong of New York vetoed the bill, it had to be repassed by the Legislature. This was no easy task; but again Platt demonstrated his mastery. Many Democrats refused to cooperate further, and the bill became a party measure. In the final roll call only 6 of the 114 Republicans in the Assembly and only one of the 36 Republicans in the Senate voted in the negative. When Andrew H. Green heard that Governor Morton had signed the measure he hurried into Platt's office and said: "I came in to express my gratitude to the Father of Greater New York." To this Platt replied: "And I desire to express my appreciation of the marvelous devotion and work of the Grandfather of Greater New York."

The law of consolidation had been written, but no one knew what the governmental forms of the new metropolis would be. Governor Morton, in May, 1896, appointed a charter commission which inspired popular confidence. Benjamin F. Tracy, who had been Secretary of the Navy under President Harrison, was named president. His associates were: Seth Low, Judge John F. Dillon and Ashbel P. Fitch from New York; Stewart L. Woodford (who was later named

TRANSMITTED to the MAYOR

MAR 25 1897

[signature]

CHAP. 378

AN ACT

To unite into one municipality under the corporate
name of The City of New York, the various communities lying in and about New York harbor,
including the city and county of New York, the
city of Brooklyn and the county of Kings, the
county of Richmond, and part of the county of
Queens, and to provide for the government
thereof.

*The People of the State of New York, represented in Senate and
Assembly, do enact as follows:*

CHAPTER I.

BOUNDARIES, BOROUGHS, POWERS, RIGHTS AND OBLIGATIONS OF
THE CITY.

THE CITY OF NEW YORK; CORPORATIONS CONSOLIDATED; TERRITORY; SHORT
TITLE OF THIS ACT.

Section 1. All the municipal and public corporations and parts of

municipal and public corporations, including cities, villages, towns

and school districts, but not including counties, within the following by President McKinley to be Minister at Madrid), Silas B. Dutcher, and William C. Dewitt from Brooklyn; Garret J. Garretson from Queens; and George M. Pinney, Jr., from Richmond. Members *ex officio,* in addition to Mayor Strong of New York, and Mayor Wurster of Brooklyn, were Andrew H. Green, Campbell W. Adams, Theodore E. Hancock, and Patrick J. Gleason. A subcommittee on draft, under the chairmanship of William C. Dewitt, began the difficult task of framing a fundamental law for a municipality of more than 3,100,000 persons, living within an area of 359 square miles; for the boundaries of the enlarged city were to include old New York and "all municipal corporations and parts of such corporations, other than counties, within the counties of Kings and Richmond, Long Island City, the towns of Newtown, Flushing and Jamaica and that part of Hempstead in Queens County, west of a line drawn from Flushing between Rockaway Beach and Shelter Island to the Ocean."

The charter commission was able to present its first draft as a "gift to the city" on Christmas morning. A small group of political leaders, including Governor Morton, Governor-elect Frank S. Black, Lieutenant-Governor Timothy C. Woodruff, and "Boss" Platt had celebrated Christmas Eve at Governor Morton's home in New York by expressing approval of the document. The legislature acted promptly, passing the bill in February, 1897. Within a few weeks Brooklyn opinion likewise accepted the charter. If surrender to New York was inevitable, the terms were unexpectedly favorable. Thankful that his earlier fears had been groundless, Mayor Wurster signed away his city's independence.

While Brooklyn rejoiced, New York denounced. Its citizens were suddenly appalled by the magnitude of the new responsibilities which they were assuming. Nothing in the charter lifted their spirits or gave promise of a happier future. Editorial writers in the *Times* and the *Tribune* pointed to confusing provisions and agreed with the Chamber of Commerce that it was difficult to see how the taxpayers of New York could profit under the new government. Ex-Mayor Hewitt and ex-Mayor Grace asked the legislature to give the charter further consideration. This view was endorsed by the Bar Association, the Real Estate Exchange, the Reform Club, the Union League Club, the City Club, and the Board of Trade and Transportation. E. L. Godkin, still writing incisively for the *Evening Post*, insisted that the charter was apt to reverse the trend toward greater democracy in American municipal government. Beneath the apparent concentration of power in the mayor's office he saw a diffusion of responsibility among boards and commissions. He doubted that effective local self-government would mark the initial years of the enlarged city.

As a member of the charter commission Mayor Strong had agreed to the charter's provisions. As Mayor of New York he sent it back to Albany with his veto and thus forced the legislature to pass it again. This proved to be a mere formality, for the lines in the legislature held, as Platt said they would. Governor Black, performing the service expected of him, signed the charter on May 4, 1897.

Perhaps the strong criticism of the structure of government was a distinct advantage to the citizens of Greater New York. They had read so much concerning the inherent weakness of a federal system resting upon the creation of the five boroughs that they expected difficulties. They had been warned so often of the administrative conflicts which might arise between the various departments and commissions that they were prepared for the necessity of charter revision.

NEW YORK WELCOMES ADMIRAL DEWEY

Aware of the experimental nature of much of the structure as well as the functioning of their new government, they were pleasantly surprised when it proved far more workable than its critics had been willing to concede. It was possible to fix power as well as responsibility in the office of mayor; and the board of estimate and apportionment developed quickly into a policy-making and finance-controlling body, emphasizing both the autonomy and the federal unity of the boroughs. Most important of all, the charter (the worst imperfections of which were cured by a thorough revision in 1901), provided the opportunity for that "imperial city" which Andrew Green had long prophesied would some day rise above the three islands at the mouth of the "lordly Hudson."

From Van Wyck to O'Dwyer

By CARL CARMER

O UT OF the dark narrows of New York streets rose a steady roaring chant. It was election in 1897 and the air was shaking with the tramp of marching men. Saloons blazed with light. Brass bands thumped and blared "A Hot Time in the Old Town Tonight."

"We told you so!" screamed the zigzagging snake-dancers. "We didn't do a thing to them, did we?"

Hoarse men climbed the steps of Manhattan's brownstone fronts to scream over the milling crowds:

"What's the matter with Van Wyck?"

"He's all right!" The yelling thousands seemed to make the walls about them tremble.

"Who's all right?"

"Van Wyck!"

Little parades were starting here and there. Bass drums— and dishpans—beat the old march rhythm.

Boom! Boom! Boom, boom, boom!

New York was no longer Little Old New York. It had become the widely spread five-boroughed metropolis—The City of Greater New York—which had elected as its first mayor Robert A. Van Wyck, little-known judge with the name of a Knickerbocker aristocrat, who had promised Tammany he would do as he was told.

ROBERT A. VAN WYCK

Tammany had taken this election seriously. Not since its foundation in 1789 as an anti-aristocratic organization to combat such exclusive societies as the Order of the Cincinnati (officers of the American Revolution whose memberships were to be inherited throughout the family generations by eldest sons) had it so yearned for victory. Not even in the days of its notorious criminal leader, "Boss" Tweed, had the prospects for the prosperity that follows the election of loyal members been brighter. The patronage of all the now consolidated boroughs, Brooklyn, Bronx, Manhattan, Queens, and Richmond, was at stake.

And Tammany had been out of power. Revelations of an investigation ordered by the State Legislature and conducted by its Lexow Committee (appointed in 1894) had disgraced the Society much as it had been disgraced in the days of Tweed. Its take from the vices of gambling and prostitution had been so large that shocked voters had elected an honest and able reform candidate, William L. Strong, to the mayoralty. Strong had given the city an admirable administration, too admirable for practical politics. Thomas C. Platt, Republican state boss, had been bitter about it. Scorning Strong's stubborn refusal to give patronage to good Republicans as attributable in large measure to his flaunting of that late nineteenth century symbol of integrity and upright citizenship, "a little bunch of whiskers under his chin," Platt had his own beard trimmed close.

Strong's appointees went on working for the public weal, disregarding their own political futures. Colonel Waring, head of the Street Cleaning Department, refused to hire deserving Republicans to wield its brooms. Police Commissioner Theodore Roosevelt acted on the theory that the Sunday Closing Law meant what it said and provided convincing documentation for his later remark: "If a reform administration honestly endeavors to carry out reform, it makes an end of itself at the end of its term."

A Republican legislature had further tormented Tammany (and set a trap for itself) first by uniting the boroughs, and second, believing that the Republicans would win the first election, by voting that the term of the mayor should be four years instead of the two to which Manhattan was accustomed. Little wonder the jaws of the Tammany Tiger dripped with appetite!

To make sure of the kill the sachems of the Tammany wigwam had called on the best brains of the Society. Back from Wantage, his charming estate in Berkshire, England, came the be-tweeded country squire, associate of princes (including Prince Edward of Wales), and follower of the sport of kings, Richard Welstead Croker, once bully-boy of the Fourth Avenue Tunnel gang. Croker had forsaken his rule of Tammany and his upstate stud farm at Richfield Springs, and with some slight portion of the millions that had come his way had purchased Wantage, announcing his permanent retirement from politics. But this was an emergency. And it had been this Irish-born Napoleon's brilliant strategy to nominate Van Wyck. He could not be easily attacked, because no one knew him or his past. His name commanded the kind of prestige accorded New York's old Dutch families. He had agreed to refer all of his decisions to the leaders of Tammany.

Opposition had been divided. Seth Low, President of Columbia University, had been a reform candidate. So had the distinguished economist Henry George, advocate of one tax only—on real estate. The Republicans had nominated Benjamin F. Tracy, a lawyer in partnership with Tom

POLICE DEPARTMENT, 1898

Platt's son. Mr. George had died during the campaign and
enough of his followers had swung to Van Wyck to do the
job. The Tammany candidate for District Attorney, Asa

[65]

Bird Gardner, had won political immortality in a campaign speech by shouting "To Hell with Reform" and the celebrators on election night were chanting that Reform had taken the suggestion.

For four years, then, Tammany held political control of the City of Greater New York—but not without evidences of coming disaster. Croker returned to Wantage after the tumult and the shouting over his triumph died and there ran the organization's affairs by cable. Rumblings of discontent reverberated through the Hall. The hearty, roistering, democratic Irish had no patience with politics conducted in absentia by an expatriate in a dress suit. The handsome, gigantic Big Tim Sullivan, darling of the Palm Pleasure Association, the Bowling Green Wheelmen, the Chop Suey Social Club, and many another happy organization, had already begun to doubt the infallibility of the "Duke of Tammany." Ridiculing Croker's insistence that politicians, desiring to confer with him after the victory of 1897, should be formally dressed in the evening, George Washington Plunkitt, Tammany prototype of Finley Peter Dunne's "Mr. Dooley," said, "You have no idea of the harm that dress-suits have done in politics. They are not so fatal to young politicians as civil service reform and drink, but they have scores of victims." William S. Devery, who, as a police captain, won undying fame in a police investigation in 1894 by answering his questioners time and again with "Touchin' on and appertainin' to that matter, I disremember," was now Chief of Police and already ungratefully fulminating revolt. Men of considerable influence in the Democratic Party demanded that Croker cease his practice of demanding, even of State Supreme Court Judges, that they appoint his nominees to courtroom jobs.

[66]

SETH LOW

While dissatisfaction brewed within the Hall, Tammany's usual Nemesis, an investigation, was being cooked up outside. It came in 1899, and with it evidence so damning that the old cycle of corruption, reform, corruption, reform was set in motion again. Croker, facing the questioners of the Mazet Committee, created by the State Legislature, found himself backed against a wall, eventually refusing to answer the most damaging of questions. Mayor Van Wyck, answering inquiries as to vice of a particularly depraved nature in the city, weakly replied that such things were not indulged in when he was a boy and that he did not believe present society was any worse than it had been then. Reports of corruption in the police department came by way of confessions by police extortioners and testimony of their victims. "We see the powers of government prostituted to protect criminals," read the Mazet report, "to demoralize the police, to debauch the public conscience and to turn governmental functions into channels for private gain." By this time even the most optimistic of the members of Tammany realized that the forces of Reform were crouching for the kill.

At the end of Tammany's four-year joy-ride with Van Wyck these forces sprang. Former reform candidate Seth Low, scion of one of Brooklyn's China trade families, resigned his presidency of Columbia and ran for the mayoralty of Greater New York, promising reform. Despite Bill Devery's scoffs at him as "Little Eva," despite Richard Croker's crafty naming of an honest Brooklyn lawyer, Edward M. Shepard, as his opponent, despite Tammany's employment of all the techniques it had learned in the rough-and-tumble of practical politics, Low was elected, and with him as District Attorney, William Travers Jerome, a vigorous and fearless prosecutor.

Again came eager, humorless reform. Pompous righteousness, no matter how honest and well-meaning, has never found favor among New York voters. With commendable understatement, District Attorney Jerome said of his former fellow candidate, "Egotism, self-complacency and constitutional timidity are not the elements to make a leader." As for Tom Platt, he continued to be horrified by the lack of practicality of Reform officials. Low's bending over backwards in not getting rid of many hundreds of Tammany officeholders he regarded as bordering on political insanity.

The legislature having again delighted Tammany by returning the office of mayor to a two-year term, the dullness of Reform did not last any longer than that. Low disregarded patronage, tried to clean up the police department, the streets, the slums. He encouraged civil service reform, education, transportation. "He came and went," Tom Platt reported, "and New York City is still the same old town."

During Seth Low's tenure of office the influence of Croker had faded. The stocky old man with the cruel green eyes and the stubby beard had lost his last battle when Low had been elected. He would win the English Derby in 1907 with his horse "Orby." He would come back—after the death of his estranged wife in 1914—to marry in the same year twenty-three-year-old Beula Edmondson. But both the bully-boy of Fourth Avenue and the squire of Wantage were political ghosts now.

With the help of Big Tim Sullivan, Charles Francis Murphy, native of the Gas House District, former catcher on a good semi-professional ball team, owner of a number of well-placed and appointed saloons, had become the acknowledged leader of Tammany Hall. Murphy had been appointed by Van Wyck to be one of the four dock commissioners of the city. After the Tammany defeat of 1901 he had organized the New York Contracting and Trucking Company which leased docks from the city and offered to rent them to customers. It turned out to be a very profitable business. Murphy was elevated to Tammany's leadership soon thereafter, and it was folk legend in political circles that he had earned his first million.

Shrewd, taciturn, ambitious, able, Charles F. Murphy was a political boss of real stature. He needed to be. The unlovable but impeccable Mr. Low was running on a Fusion

Ticket for reelection, and Bill Devery, the former police chief with the conveniently faulty memory, had become an anti-Low, anti-Tammany maverick, running on a ticket of his own and prophesying that this time "the downtrod will rise in their might and . . . make the Charley Murphys . . . look like calico dogs stuffed with saloon sweepings."

Remembering the dissatisfaction of the rank and file with Croker's insistence on dress suits as evening wear, Devery ridiculed Murphy's associations with men of social pretensions, dubbing him "Sir Charles" and suggesting that he would soon be wearing a monocle like his friends of the *bon ton.*

"Since Charlie Murphy has got to running with S. Sergeant Cram," he said, "he's turned up his trousers at the bottom. . . . Instead of being a gas-house boy and dressing like one, he goes over on Fifth Avenue every day."

The campaign contributed much to Murphy's political education. To make his effort as the man mounted on the Tiger seem an easy triumph, he had scheduled as candidate a charming gentleman, George B. McClellan, a scholar who was later to be an effective college professor, a man in whose veins ran the blood of a Civil War hero. To make assurance doubly sure, the boss then offered Tammany's endorsement to the Fusionists' candidates for comptroller and president of the Board of Aldermen. These gentlemen, both men of proven efficiency and conscience, found the offer flattering and accepted. It would seem that now it was only necessary to await the election returns with calm. Suddenly a storm blew up and Mr. Murphy's protective umbrella turned inside out. The Fusionists denounced their candidates for accepting Tammany support, and the Democrats of Brooklyn denounced them also as unfit for Democratic candidacy.

GEORGE B. MC CLELLAN

Murphy had to work much harder than he had at first planned, but Low's unpopularity was working with him and McClellan was elected.

Two years later he was reelected, despite the entrance into city politics of the crusading young newspaper owner William Randolph Hearst. Hearst, having organized the Municipal Ownership League to oppose a Tammany grab for traction graft, had tried to persuade Judge William J. Gaynor to accept its nomination for mayor, but, failing in that, had decided to run himself. Radicals, progressives, and thousands of workers marched under his banners, shouting in rhythmic unison, "Hearst! Hearst! Hearst!" His papers carried screaming headlines denouncing Charles Murphy as a criminal in business and politics. One ran a cartoon depicting the Tammany boss in convict stripes with the caption: "Look Out, Murphy! It's a Short Lockstep from Delmonico's to Sing Sing."

When the returns were in, showing McClellan the winner over Hearst by a plurality of only 3,500 votes, the publisher at once demanded a recount, alleging that the election had been stolen. Hysterically his supporters charged, when the recount had been made, that Tammany had stuffed the ballot boxes before recounting began. The Hearst papers continued their vilification of Murphy as an arch-criminal throughout the year 1905, and their owner was quite as violent in his public utterances.

And at Buffalo in 1906, by one of the cynical ironies of political intrigue, Charles Murphy, who had been seeking to extend his power over the party throughout the state, proved that he had done so by dictating the nomination of Hearst for the governorship on the Democratic ticket. When Tammany could nominate a possible governor of New York State, it was beginning to appear, through the astuteness of Murphy, not municipal but national in its influence. The new boss, scorning the Croker days when control of city government and the rewards to be derived therefrom were enough, had set his sights higher than even his immediate associates had dreamed.

But Charles Evans Hughes was elected governor. Murphy suffered minor city defeats also. His espousal of Hearst had alienated Mayor McClellan who, having made one of the best appointments ever made by a New York mayor, that of John Purroy Mitchel (nephew of Fire Commissioner Henry D. Purroy) to be Assistant Corporation Counsel, gave that young lawyer opportunity to make a name for himself in investigations of the activities of the presidents of the Boroughs of Manhattan, the Bronx, and Queens. Mitchel conducted the proceedings so ably that two were removed from office, and one, feeling the imperative urgency of a European trip, resigned. Mitchel, New Yorkers felt, would be heard from again.

Determined that Tammany should keep the leadership now foundering under McClellan, Charles Murphy looked for a candidate who would unquestionably be elected. That man was at hand, but from Tammany's point of view he had two faults. The first was that he was stoutly defiant of organized discipline, the second that he was so able and honest that he was looked upon with great favor by anti-Tammany fusion forces, including Hearst's adherents, as their prospective candidate. Even the Republicans considered the redoubtable Judge William J. Gaynor, a Democrat, as acceptable, providing he would renounce Tammany support. This Gaynor refused to do. The Fusion and Republican parties found themselves in the embarrassing dilemma of wishing to nominate on an anti-Tammany ticket a man who would not declare that he was anti-Tammany. If they had been willing to nominate him without exacting a pledge, it is probable that Charles Murphy would have made the nomination unanimous and an unpleasant campaign which went to extremes of vilification would have been avoided.

But since Gaynor would not attack Tammany, the Republicans nominated an admirable, public-spirited citizen, Otto T. Bannard. Tammany then nominated Gaynor; and Hearst, disappointed in both candidates, reluctantly decided he would again represent the party for which he had run before, now known as the Civic Alliance. Gaynor, feeling betrayed by Hearst, who he said had guaranteed him support, denounced the publisher bitterly. Hearst, ignoring the fact that he had been a Murphy-Tammany candidate for governor, called Gaynor a tool of Tammany and its despicable and dishonest leader. He hired as an aide in the campaign William M. Ivins, who had been the negligible Republican candidate for mayor in the previous election, and Ivins fought with no holds barred. He attacked the judge, whose integrity had been acknowledged by all parties before the campaign, as having sold out to corrupt Tammany. He charged that Gaynor's private life left much to be desired and that his past held shady and disreputable incidents.

Actually William J. Gaynor was not only honest and capable, but one of those few seekers of public office who have within them elements of greatness. Reared in Unionville, New York, he had the typical experiences of an Oneida County farm boy—the chores, the one-room school, fishing in the Oriskany, the Sequoit, the Unadilla, wandering beside the wide Mohawk, learning to swim in the Erie Canal. When William was thirteen the family moved to near-by Utica where the boy, in 1864, entered the Assumption Academy of the Christian Brothers. A fine scholar and a man of deeply religious nature, he became a member of this teaching Brother-

WILLIAM J. GAYNOR

hood. The principal of the Utica school took him to visit the St. Louis, Missouri, chapter of the order, where in long black cassock and flat hat with a wide brim, William Gaynor taught for a year under the name of Brother Hadrian. Soon afterwards he forsook all association with formalized and institutional religion, though he never abandoned his deeply religious convictions.

By 1874 he was a young lawyer in Brooklyn performing the silliest act of his life, his personal arrest of Theodore

[75]

Tilton on the charge that Tilton had libeled the famous Brooklyn minister Henry Ward Beecher, by publishing in the Brooklyn *Eagle* his side of the scandal involving Beecher with Mrs. Tilton. But soon thereafter Gaynor's career found its lodestar and he became a fearless champion of the people. The citizens of Brooklyn recognized his impatience with stupidity, his wrath at wrongdoing, and honored him. He was consistently the enemy of special privilege, the friend of civil rights. He had supported the creation of Greater New York. By 1909 his bitter attacks on bossism and his originality, common sense, and humanity as expressed in his decisions as a Supreme Court Judge, had brought him such prominence that he had been seriously considered as a candidate for the vice-presidency.

Had William Gaynor consistently acted on the philosophy he believed, he would have achieved true greatness. It was a tragic defect in his character that his temper flared when others attacked him. "I make no personal attack on anybody, nor will I answer any attack," he said in serene and philosophic reply to charges made by Ivins, but answering other defamations, shouted: "Shut up, you slanderers, you blackguards, you mud slingers. . . . Even though you bespatter me I shall not turn to answer."

The New York *Evening World,* heartily supporting Gaynor, was yet constrained to describe him as "irascible, suspicious, vituperative." When the *World,* cleverly building circulation, invited Arthur Brisbane, Hearst's famous editor, to attack Gaynor in its columns, the judge promptly sued the *World* for printing Brisbane's words. The *World* then generously argued that a candidate who would sue a supporting newspaper during his campaign would certainly be independent when in office.

"No organization made me and, by the Eternal, none will ever pull me down," said Gaynor, answering the critics of his Tammany candidacy. In Tammany Hall itself he confounded his listeners by beginning his speech with, "And so this is Tammany Hall . . . I did not even know where it was . . . where is the Tiger?—that Tiger which they say is going to swallow me up—if there happen to be any swallowing up, it is not at all unlikely I may be on the outside of the Tiger." And the people of the City of Greater New York believed him, for when the votes had been counted, only one of all the candidates of Boss Murphy had been elected, the one whom they knew Murphy could not boss—the Mayor. The City of Greater New York, after more than a decade of helpless and inconsistent political floundering had at last chosen a chief executive who was distinguished, honest, and at the same time an effective public servant.

The administration that followed was miraculous in raising the government of New York from the mire of contempt in which it was held by the cities of the world, and yet it was as full of inconsistencies and contradictions as the character of William J. Gaynor. Six months after it began, the *Evening World* stated: "No other man ever accomplished so much in so little time. He has revolutionized the spirit of the city government. The power of his precept and example has spread throughout the public service."

Fortunately furnished by the anti-Tammany forces with Fusion-elected officers of honesty, intelligence, and efficiency, Mayor Gaynor added others of like quality by his wise and independent appointments. His interest in the welfare of the masses whose government he led evinced itself in his immediate suppression of police brutalities, his enthusiastic espousal of recreational facilities for children, his angry denials of special privilege to those who assumed it, his understanding sympathy with the poor and the unfortunate.

During the same six months he had proved himself a petty tyrant among the employees of his own office, and at an Associated Press dinner at the Waldorf Astoria Hotel had denounced Hearst as a libeler and a forger, thereby denying the teachings of one of his oft-quoted philosophers, Marcus Aurelius, who urged men "to live without anger in the midst of lying and unjust men."

In the summer of 1910, planning a European holiday, the Mayor reserved passage on the liner *Kaiser Wilhelm*. While saying farewell to a few members of his official family on the deck of that ship he was shot and severely wounded by a crazed former employee of the city. The bullet lodged in the roof of his pharynx and was never removed. By October he had recovered enough to be back at his job, announcing on his return, "I forgive everybody everything every night. Let not the sun go down on my wrath." He immediately plunged into the work he had so successfully begun, but the bullet had not disciplined his temper. Nor was it improved by the fact that public apologies for intemperate remarks about former Police Commissioner Bingham and Judge James W. Gerard (later Ambassador to Germany) were wrung from him by these gentlemen. Complaints of reformers irked him and set off verbal fireworks. When the pastor of the Madison Square Presbyterian Church, Dr. Charles H. Parkhurst, whom he regarded as a meddling, sensation-mongering, professional reformer, attacked him on his handling of the city police, the Mayor said of him, "He thinks he is pious, when he is only bilious."

Despite all these evidences of a choleric disposition, the Mayor got things done. He waged successful campaigns for

CHARLES F. MURPHY IN TAMMANY HALL

Brown Brothers

better housing, improved education, inspection of weights and measures, sanitation, inspection of foods, and the more expert care of women in child birth. So busy and enthusiastic was he that when it was suggested to him that nomination on the Democratic ticket for the governorship of the state was his for the asking, Gaynor refused to consider it, even though he and the rest of America knew that it might lead to the Presidency.

Tammany in the meanwhile was grumpily nursing its wounds. Its one elected candidate had been worse than useless to it. When Gaynor had been asked, after election, what should be done for "Boss" Murphy who had given him the nomination, he had replied, after a long pause, "Suppose that we give him a few kind words." Tammany could not grow fat on words, and some of its leaders and its rank and file were seeking revenue from activities not approved officially by the Hall, among them gambling and prostitution. Big Tim Sullivan, who had included himself in good company by announcing in his one campaign speech in the fall of 1909, "I'm not the first man who has been pilloried between thieves," had become the close friend of a gambler named Herman Rosenthal, who was paying large sums to the police for protection. Rosenthal, while denying that Big Tim was his partner in gambling, admitted that the politician had lent him $2,000 to help finance his gambling partnership with Lieutenant Charles Becker, head of Police Commissioner Rhinelander Waldo's vice squad. When Charles S. Whitman, the district attorney, requested proof of these facts which had already been reported to the *Evening World,* Rosenthal made an appointment for the purpose of supplying complete data. In the early morning of the July day before that appointment, Rosenthal was murdered by hired gunmen in front of the Hotel Metropole. Five policemen stationed within a hundred yards of the spot, near 43d Street and Broadway, were not active enough to apprehend the murderers, who roared away in a gray automobile. At once Charles Whitman, efficient and ambitious, went into action.

It was obvious that behind this brazen crime lay the sinister fact of police corruption. This, Mayor Gaynor, who had strenuously fought to build an honest Police Department, refused to admit. He seemed to resent Whitman's activity as if it were a part of a plot to embarrass him. As the people of the city wrathfully demanded that something be done, Gaynor stubbornly did nothing. He indifferently refused to see the palpable truth and called Whitman and all those who supported him scandalmongers. A situation which he would have fought tooth and nail, had he discovered it, he regarded as non-existent because he was sure that he had already destroyed all vestiges of alliance between vice and the police.

But Whitman found a witness who remembered the number on the license plate of the murder car. Bit by bit he advanced the solution of the murder. He found the occupants of the car, and a horrified and fascinated public became aware of the inner workings of gangsterdom. Jack Rose, little bald gambler who gave the evidence that convicted Becker, became so widely known that a cocktail was named after him. Leftie Louie, Gyp the Blood, Whitey Lewis, Dago Frankie, became household words. They all died in the electric chair at Sing Sing. So did their employer, Lieutenant Charles Becker. And Big Tim Sullivan, the gamblers' friend, went crazy.

An investigation of the Police Department was inevitable. Judge Henry H. Curran, chairman of the investigating com-

[81]

mittee of aldermen, has described what happened before it, in his admirably frank memoir *Pillar to Post*. Mayor Gaynor refused to cooperate. "I cannot ally myself with you in any effort to discover wrongdoing in the police department," he wrote. "I have devoted much of my life to efforts to lift government up and make it respectable and honest, and I intend to continue in that work, but I have never allied myself in it with anyone who was not himself above reproach. I have called attention to the miserable grafting carried on by members of the Board of Aldermen in respect to the licensing of newsstands. I have no doubt that the Aldermen who do this share in the extortion of money."

Curran immediately sued the Mayor for libel and the Mayor had the Alderman's record carefully searched. To a friend who reported him honest, Gaynor replied, "He's an alderman—he can't be honest"; but soon the city was aware that its testy chief executive had again been forced into the humiliation of writing a public letter of apology.

The most important considerations of Mayor Gaynor's last year of office were the contracts for building new subways. At first a believer in municipal ownership, he had changed his mind and then changed it again. His vacillation caused criticism which he answered by quoting Gladstone, "Wise men change their minds, fools do not." His final decision was a bitterly attacked compromise—dual contracts under which the existing companies were to provide aid in financing the work of building and to operate the new lines. "Tammany would not dare give any corporation what these eminently respectable gentlemen are giving to Morgan and Belmont and this traction monopoly," said Gaynor's usual champion, the *Evening World*.

The Mayor, now sixty-two years old, was tiring. The

would-be assassin's bullet had weakened him. His constant battling with both evil and well-meaning opponents had aged him. "Learn to be resigned and content, whatever may happen," had been his favorite saying throughout his life, yet the old warrior must go down fighting. As his administration ended he knew that he would have no organized support for renomination. Tammany had suffered too long under the indifference which it regarded as ingratitude. His failure to cooperate with Whitman, his frequently inconsistent and stubborn antipathies, had alienated the anti-Tammany Fusionists. Only Charles Murphy, at a meeting of the Tammany leaders at Delmonico's Restaurant, was willing to consider renominating him, yet, characteristically, Gaynor considered the "Boss" his arch-betrayer. He stood alone, unnominated. To the City Hall reporters, whom he had long known, he said a few words summing up his service to the city. In conclusion he said, "I have had a pretty hard time for four years to hold my own against all comers, and against every corrupt influence, but I have been mayor."

Again he sought rest in Europe. The day before he left, a loyal Citizens Committee informed him that they had nominated him for Mayor. Weak and tottering, he climbed the steps of City Hall. His secretary read his speech of acceptance, which ended, "The people of the city are going to shovel all of these miserable little political grafters into one common dumpheap."

On board the liner *Baltic* he said to his bodyguard: "I am going where they can't get at me." Five days before he died, he sent a wireless message from out on the waters calling on New York voters not to throw the government of the city "into the control of a vulgar gang of grafters, all of one stripe such as met at Delmonico's."

His last words to the people whom he had served were verses about them.

> Give them the shovel

he wrote, referring to the building of the subways,

> No king, no clown
> Shall rule this town.
> That day has gone forever.

In the following months it almost seemed that the learned old Mayor's prophecy was coming true. Tammany's candidate, Edward E. McCall, was overwhelmed by an avalanche of votes for Fusion's white knight, John Purroy Mitchel, and Mitchel's administration was, from its beginning, a legend of well-nigh perfect government. Gaynor's four years of establishing efficient procedures and insisting on their honest and intelligent use had prepared the way for a champion, and the champion was ready. Like Gaynor, John Purroy Mitchel was of Irish blood, but the distance between the farm on the banks of Oriskany Creek and the suburban lot in Fordham on the Bronx was more than geographical. Mitchel's grandfather, famous Irish rebel-patriot, had been a convict sentenced for his political activities to Van Diemen's Land, whence he had escaped to America. There he had reared a brood of rebel heroes, for in the War between the States one son, a Confederate officer, was killed while in command of Fort Sumter, another died gallantly in Pickett's charge at Gettysburg, and the third, John Purroy Mitchel's father, was a captain on the staff of Stonewall Jackson.

Captain James Mitchel sent his son John to public school and thence to St. John's College for his early education. He entered Columbia University in 1895 and soon thereafter began to develop those traits which made a legend of him be-

Brown Brothers

JOHN PURROY MITCHEL, WITH THEODORE
ROOSEVELT AND CHARLES EVANS HUGHES

fore he died. He was tall and long-legged, but quick in movement. He was a good boxer in college and an even better
fencer. He walked swiftly and gracefully, and had a quick,
birdlike turn of the head which people remembered as characteristic. His personality was both ingratiating and com-
pelling. Few could resist his grin and the understanding
humor in his brown eyes. There was also a kind of devil-may-

[85]

care insouciance about him, a lack of concern over what might happen to him, which was at once his chief charm and his major fault.

Appointed Assistant Corporation Counsel by Mayor McClellan he had, while still in his twenties, won his political spurs by investigating Tammany's borough presidents out of office. At thirty, as a Fusion candidate, he was elected President of the Board of Aldermen, and his first act was to tell the Board that the best action it could take would be to abolish itself.

Mitchel was thirty-five when elected Mayor, the youngest man to hold the office in New York history.

"To my mind there is only one course to pursue," he said. *"Be right and speak out."* This was easier to say than to do, but Mitchel had a remarkable ability for being right without being self-conscious or priggish about it. His appointments were particularly fitting, for he had the kind of sensitivity that enabled him to pick exactly the right man for the office he was filling. Some of Mayor Gaynor's appointees were able and honest—as in the case of Police Commissioner Waldo—without being at all suited to their jobs. Of Mitchel, who was a Democrat, Republican ex-President Theodore Roosevelt said in 1917: "He has the invaluable quality of choosing and being able to command the services of the finest and best men of the city. I wish to Heaven it were possible to say of all national administrations that they would get, and could get, men of the kind that John Purroy Mitchel puts into high places." Among the men whom the young Mayor chose to have about him were Elbert H. Gary, Chairman of the Mayor's Unemployment Committee, Cornelius Vanderbilt III, Chairman of the Mayor's Committee for Defense (succeeded, when Vanderbilt entered active military service, by Willard Straight), Henry L. Stimson, Cleveland Dodge, George Wickersham, and Jacob Schiff. Perhaps the best of all his appointments was that of Arthur Woods as Police Commissioner. What Waldo had failed to do with Gaynor's support, Woods did swiftly, quietly, and effectively.

The Fire Department was equally well handled; and there were distinct improvements in the management of schools and of prisons. When the administration of Roman Catholic charities was questioned, Mitchel, himself a Catholic, courageously declared that they should be as carefully examined as any non-sectarian organization.

As war threatened, Mitchel was the eager patriot, a strenuous advocate of preparedness. He attended the first civilian training camp at Plattsburg in 1915. Long before the fateful spring of 1917 he was demanding national preparedness. When he felt that State Senator Robert L. Wagner was needlessly delaying the Federal Government's acquisition of property needed for coast defense, he spoke out: "It would seem that there are some members of the Legislature working more in the interests of Germany than in the interests of the United States."

It was such forthright but politically inadvisable utterances as this which led Elihu Root to say of Mitchel after his death, "Some of the strong enmities which prevented his re-election would have been avoided if it had not been that he was so little concerned about what was going to happen to him personally." This disregard of self was showing in other ways. Tennis had taken the place of fencing, and he was a strenuous player but likely to become overheated in a close match and leave the court without remembering to put on a coat. He loved to drive his automobile at high speed—a sport that has hazards of its own.

[87]

The dress suit, too, was doing the deadly work that Tammany's old-timer, George Washington Plunkitt, had attributed to it. The Mayor was a more than welcome guest at the dinner tables of the Vanderbilts and others in the first ranks of New York's social elite. Oswald Garrison Villard, owner of *The Nation,* and a hard-to-satisfy campaigner for civic good, could find but one fault with him. After Mitchel's untimely death, in an article signed O. G. V., this veteran warrior for democratic virtue wrote:

It is, however, undeniably true that Mr. Mitchel was not at bottom a real democrat, and he played into the hands of his enemies by his inability to go among the plain people and make it clear to them that he was their mayor and was working solely in their interests. Regrettably, too, there constantly appeared items about the Mayor's appearance in high society. . . . His proper friendship with the Vanderbilts, as well as his attendance at dances, was exploited to his extreme detriment.

No mayor ever deserved more from the people of his city. But Tammany had been starving for patronage for two long terms and it was determined to win. Mitchel's own friends unwisely aided the opposition by contributing to his second campaign a "slush fund" of no less than two million dollars. The Mayor's excitable patriotism also had unfortunate repercussions. He followed his attack on Senator Wagner with another on Tammany's nominee, "Red Mike" Hylan, a run-of-the-mill organization man, accusing him of having pro-German leanings. His political nonchalance and lack of foresight led to resounding defeat. In 1913 he had polled 57 percent of the total vote. In 1917 he received only 24 percent.

On July 6, 1918, at Camp Gerstner, Lake Charles, Louisiana, Major John Purroy Mitchel was killed in the service of

Brown Brothers

JOHN F. HYLAN

his country. He had suffered from excruciating headaches and had been heard to say: "If I get a real bad headache while up in the clouds, it will be all over with me." He had been in the clouds and he had fallen.

The shrewd Mr. Murphy, given to taking no avoidable chances, saw to it that no blunder marked his 1917 campaign against John Purroy Mitchel. Since Mitchel had not been popular in Queens, Brooklyn, the Bronx, and Richmond, the boss asked the Democratic leaders of these boroughs for suggestions. Inasmuch as Mitchel, though a Roman Catholic, had criticized the management of certain Catholic charities, it was essential, Murphy said, that a loyal Catholic

be nominated. "Big Jim" Sinnott, Brooklyn leader, had just
the man in mind—John F. Hylan, for many years a judge in
the County Court. Hylan had a background, Murphy soon
discovered, that furnished excellent campaign material. He
had been a farm boy in a little town in the Catskills. At the
age of nineteen he had set out for New York, where he arrived with but $1.50 in his pocket and the farewell words
of his mother to guide him: "Be honest, be truthful, be upright, and do to others as you would have them do to you."

Hylan got a job on the elevated railroad, and after nine
years became an engineer at $15 a week. Then he married
his mountain sweetheart, Marian O'Hara, who urged him
to become a lawyer. After he passed his bar examinations,
he discovered that Brooklyn was entitled to two more magistrates than it then possessed, and persuaded Mayor McClellan to appoint him as one of them. He had served faithfully
if somewhat colorlessly ever since. Tammany saw in him an
ideal people's candidate against that aristocratic hobnobber
with the Vanderbilts, the correct Mr. Mitchel.

With the blessing of Charles Murphy and a wild hulla-
balloo of support from the papers of William Randolph
Hearst, who hated Mitchel, "Red Mike" Hylan triumphed
magnificently. Tammany's cup was soon running over, for
Hylan was no indifferent independent like Gaynor, who had
ignored his sponsors. Murphy, though famed for his silence in
such matters, was so moved by Hylan's appointments that
he remarked: "No Tammany mayor has ever been more liberal to Tammany in the matter of patronage." Nor had any
leader of Tammany been more careful than Murphy in his
suggestions as to appointees. Hylan was not a brilliant man,
nor did he have exceptional judgment, yet the Tammany officials who worked with him did reasonably well. Republican-

.Brown Brothers

PRESIDENT AND MRS. WILSON WITH MAYOR HYLAN

instigated investigations that followed the election, though
ably conducted, found little of which to complain.

Hylan worked hard. His campaign as candidate of the
masses had convinced him that he was their champion
against the disgracefully rich, the soulless corporations of
Wall Street, the powerful advocates of special privilege.
Each day he toiled from nine to six, trying desperately to
master his job. He was blundering, uncertain, and suspicious,
but filled with a sense of his own importance. The business
of the great city dragged on—with little corruption and no
spirit. At the end of the first term in 1921 he campaigned

again as "The People's Mayor" and won with a tremendous plurality of more than 400,000.

A lethargy seemed to have settled upon the city. Not much went wrong, not much was done. Writers spoke of the Hylan administration as dreary, inactive, and dull.

When Hylan heard in St. Patrick's Cathedral the high requiem Mass for the soul of Charles Murphy he knew that, with his best friend dead, his own career as the people's champion was in danger. Political authority over Tammany had fallen to Governor Al Smith, and the new arrangements would not be the same. The Mayor knew that he could more safely depend on the sixty thousand people lining Fifth Avenue than the political dignitaries about him.

The danger was not long in materializing. George W. Olvany, graduate of the Law School of New York University and Judge of the Court of General Sessions, succeeded Murphy as leader of Tammany. Acting for Al Smith, the new head of the Hall prepared for repudiation of the Mayor who had been praised by his predecessor for giving it so much patronage.

There was much talk of the "New Tammany" now. Al Smith, proving himself so worthy a Governor that he would soon be nominated for the Presidency, Robert F. Wagner, Senator of unquestionable ability and integrity, George Olvany, college-bred judge and literary defender of the Hall in high-brow magazines, were all evidence of a new spirit in the organization. "I state with positive conviction," wrote Olvany in *World's Work,* "that New York is the best governed city in the world."

But the "People's Mayor" did not seem to fit into this new fellowship. Judge Olvany had already found a smoother, brighter, younger candidate and Hylan was on the way

[92]

GOVERNOR ALFRED E. SMITH AT THE
POLLS, PUBLIC SCHOOL NO. 1

Brown Brothers

out. Wrathfully the Mayor protested against being thrown
"into the ash can." He said he would run as an independent
and hoped wistfully for the Republican nomination. It went
to a short, fiery, able little alderman named La Guardia.
Some of Hylan's former supporters stuck by him, notably
his oldest and best friend, John H. McCooey, Democratic
boss of Brooklyn. In that borough, which Hylan had served
as judge for many years, his candidacy was attacked by
Al Smith. Hylan retorted that what Governor Smith said

[93]

was "apple-sauce and venom." Smart young James J. Walker was attacking his record on subway construction, new schools, improvement of street traffic, garbage disposal, and hospital reform. Hylan knew that he could be elected if it were not for Tammany's repudiation, and he brooded over his betrayal. He apparently considered withdrawing his candidacy in favor of La Guardia, and then, in a pet because the Republicans had not nominated him, came out for Walker. In the same year he was afflicted by a stroke, from the effects of which he later died.

James J. Walker had for fifteen years fought Tammany's battles in the New York State Legislature when he was rewarded by the nomination for Mayor of New York City. In that time, aided by a quick wit and a flair for being conspicuous, he had made many friends and not all of them of his own party. He seemed to be an ideal candidate for the Hall to substitute for the ponderous Hylan. "Jimmy," as the electorate immediately called him, was nothing if not bright. A city child, brought up on the southwest edges of Greenwich Village, he had early learned to use his wits. His father had been a well-to-do lumber merchant and politician, and from him Jimmy absorbed a political outlook. He also loved and understood showmanship with all of its warrings for position and its mawkish sentimentalities. When Jimmy was still a youngster he yearned both for the footlights of Broadway and the ephemeral honors of Tin Pan Alley. He even wrote a typical popular song, "Will You Love Me in December as You Do in May?" which, because of his later political prominence, lived to plague him when his life proved no example of the virtues extolled by the words of the song.

Walker was elected by a Tammany landslide at the height of New York's prohibition joy-ride. The people of the town

JAMES J. WALKER OPENS THE SEASON AT THE POLO GROUNDS

loved him because he represented the sophistication, the freedom from stuffy Victorian principle, and the disregard of dull respectability which they themselves were feeling in the post-war, gin-made-in-the-bathtub years. National Prohibition was unenforceable in the great city and it had led to a topsy-turvy set of values in which gangster bootleggers had considerable political influence and were frequently received with admiration into the company of men and women who fancied themselves as ranking high in the city's polite society.

[95]

Jimmy's antics delighted his ever-widening constituency. The people loved his Broadway manner and Broadway talk. They loved his police escorts and his low, shiny Duesenberg automobile and his unconcealed and unconventional private life. They loved the parades to celebrate this and that—parades in which on occasion His Honor the Mayor, be-spatted, be-caned and be-highhatted, strolled jauntily, waving to his friends, wisecracking from the side of his mouth.

Receptions for visiting celebrities, some hardly worthy of the honor bestowed, were regarded as entertaining diversions by the townsfolk who lined the streets and crowded about the steps of City Hall. The civic-minded Mr. Whalen, returned from trade to public service under a mayor more congenial than Hylan, performed the duties of Chairman of the Reception Committee with an air of assurance. These doings cost a lot of money, but money was easy in the city and taxpayers liked the show and were willing to pay for it.

During Walker's first term of office he was generally approved as a mayor as well as showman. He made a trip to Europe where the crowds marveled at the slim and youthful appearance of a great American politico and applauded his wisecracks in an Americanese which our English cousins could not understand. There was no question about the warmth of his heart when the welfare of the poor and particularly of their children was concerned. Even so distinguished a writer on public affairs as Henry F. Pringle suggested in an article entitled "America's Mayor-at-Large" that, much against Jimmy's natural desires, he might be forced by public demand to leave the gay city he loved for the dull Dutch dignity of Albany and the responsibilities of the governorship. When the explosive, honest, somewhat comic La Guardia ran again for the mayoralty, the volatile, easygoing Walker defeated him handily.

Perhaps Mayor Walker's main difficulty lay in the fact that he "went along." A creature of Tammany, he made the appointments that Tammany asked, knowing that in many cases they were bad, but mistakenly trusting that he would not have to pay the penalty. All about him there was an atmosphere of great wealth easily obtained. Many a broker "took care" of a personal friend by investing on the rising market without troubling his friend to put up the funds. Fortunes were being made, on paper at least, and there seemed to be nothing even questionable in the transactions. When one small boy didn't see how his delightful friend, the Mayor, could get along on a salary of $25,000, the boy's father made investments that increased the income considerably, and Mayor Walker was amiably gratified.

But the wave was reaching the shore. Beneath the surface which the graceful figure rode so nonchalantly were obstacles that would soon force a crashing break. In Albany the shrewd Long Island Republican leader, W. Kingsland Macy, was plotting to bring about the usual investigation which upstate Republicans are glad to saddle on a Tammany administration of New York. By adroit maneuvering he got it, and with wisdom and irony chose Judge Samuel Seabury, a Democrat of background, respectability, achievement and ability that few would dare to question. The result was an exposé of such barefaced political chicanery as even Mr. Macy had not foreseen. To this day those who love the City of New York wince at the mention of the Seabury Investigation. The revelations of the Walpurgisnacht of corruption which it uncovered were both shameful and wildly comic. As the officeholder admitted his accumulation of large sums of money in manners inexplicable, some witnesses snarling, some naïvely friendly, the public was alternately shocked and wryly amused. "Tin boxes" became the folk-symbols of graft without telltale bookkeeping, and the story of the thirty-three McQuades who were dependent upon the complicated "borrowings" of the benevolent head of the family became the accepted example of all double-talk explanations.

When Judge Seabury finally put the Mayor of New York City on the stand the tragi-comedy of Jimmy Walker reached its climax and neared its end. The debonair mayor, voluble but unconvincing, made a poor witness for himself. As his story unwound, those who listened were embarrassed because it revealed the gradual deterioration of a character of more than ordinary gifts. When Russell Sherwood, the Mayor's secretary, fled to Mexico to avoid being questioned, the jig of the twenties was up. After a lame appearance before Governor Roosevelt in Albany, whither he had been summoned to give reason why he should not be removed from office, James J. Walker resigned the office generally considered second in importance in the United States and hastily departed for Europe.

As the Walkers set out for the Riviera, the President of the Board of Aldermen, Joseph V. McKee, assumed the duties of Mayor. No holder of political office in the big city was better qualified. A protégé of the gentlemanly, college-bred boss of the Bronx, Edward J. Flynn, he was a man of even greater cultural background and achievement than his sponsor. A former instructor at Fordham University and holder of the earned degree of Doctor of Laws from that institution, he had been a correspondent for both the New York *Times* and the New York *Herald,* and had written an historical volume which had been adopted by the city schools. Intelligent, idealistic, and eager to serve, he at once won the approval of both press and public by instituting reforms in the direction of economy. It

JOSEPH V. MC KEE

began to look as if Flynn's man from the Bronx would, through
the pressure of popular opinion, be the next mayor.

Tammany had other plans, however. Edward J. Flynn was not in high favor with the Hall and it had no intention of letting him have further power. When the nominations were made for the remaining year of Walker's unexpired term, Tammany named John Patrick O'Brien, one of the Surrogates of New York County, and Flynn, believing that the times called for unity in the Democratic Party, seconded the nomination, making (as he frankly says in his fascinating autobiography, *You're the Boss*) a mistake. "I have felt since," writes Mr. Flynn, "that this was the one time in my life when I did not remain true to what I actually believed. . . . I should have followed my own best judgment instead of listening to my friends."

John Patrick O'Brien was elected, but so incensed were the voters at Tammany's desertion of McKee that the Acting-Mayor received a write-in vote of over two hundred thousand as well as an extra evidence of good will in the unsuccessful efforts of more than a hundred thousand voters to write correct ballots for him.

In the regular election that followed a year later, Mr. Flynn belatedly organized a new party which he called the Recovery Party and nominated Joseph V. McKee to run against Tammany's O'Brien and the fiery La Guardia, now the candidate of both the Republican and the Fusion parties. In the one year of his service as mayor, Mr. O'Brien, honest but unimaginative, completely the obedient member of a political machine, stumbled and bungled so badly that he became a sort of caricature of all the inept and awkward men who hold offices too big for their abilities. At such times a hostile press is merciless, and O'Brien was ridiculed perhaps more than actual circumstances warranted. The nomination of McKee split the Democratic support but not as much as it split the support

JOHN P. O'BRIEN

of independent voters and reform advocates. La Guardia and McKee, realizing that the choice lay between them, ignored O'Brien as the ineffective candidate he undoubtedly was, and competed with each other in demanding the defeat of Tammany and thoroughgoing reorganization and reform. La Guardia won.

Fiorello La Guardia became a legend in his own lifetime. Now, after his death, he seems alive because of the legend's vitality.

They called him "Butch." They called him "Little Flower." They called him "The Hat." Waves of laughter swept the movie theaters when the stout short figure under the broad brim of a black Stetson appeared in the newsreels, the button-bright eyes flashing with eager sincerity, the round face working with deep emotion, the high voice squeaking in righteous indignation. But the laughter held such affection as has been accorded to few public figures.

The people of New York knew he was one of them, and that he fought their battles with everything he had. If John Purroy Mitchel had been their plumed knight, La Guardia was their Don Quixote, and when he tilted at windmills he sometimes won. He was at once an epitome of the frustrations of each poor and insignificant citizen and a symbol of the fact that in a democracy no citizen is, politically speaking, poor or insignificant.

The blood of fighters flowed in him. A grandfather battled through Italy with Garibaldi's Red Shirts and married a descendant of a Jewish refugee from the Spanish Inquisition. La Guardia's father, who joined the United States Army after coming to this country as accompanist for the great soprano Adelina Patti, was bandmaster of the 11th United States Infantry and became one of the many casualties of the deadly "embalmed beef" served at Tampa in the days of the Spanish War of '98.

Though Fiorello La Guardia was born in New York City,

FIORELLO LA GUARDIA ADDRESSES A CONFERENCE OF MAYORS *Brown Brothers*

his "home town," if the term may be defined as "the place where a man grows up," was Prescott, Arizona. It was typical of the frontier army-post villages. Cowboys and Indians and soldiers were accepted commonplaces of its simple life. Its schools were excellent. The family subscribed to the New York *World* in order to be informed on events of national and international importance, and it was from the editorials of that journal in the 90s that young Fiorello obtained a lasting distaste for Tammany.

Fiorello La Guardia tried to enlist in the war against Spain but was rejected as too young. It was hard to convince the editor of the St. Louis *Post Dispatch* that he should make a sixteen-year-old boy an accredited correspondent, but Fiorello did it and set out to accompany his father. Thanks to Tampa's bad beef, neither reached Cuba. The elder La Guardia was honorably discharged with a small pension and brought his whole family together under a New York roof. In 1901 he died.

In 1912, young Fiorello, who had garnered experience as American Consul at Fiume (then part of Hungary), as interpreter at Ellis Island, as a student in the night sessions of New York University Law School, hung out the shingle of F. H. La Guardia, Attorney-at-Law.

After two years of enthusiastic it unpaid work in behalf of the garment workers, then on strike, the new lawyer was given the nomination for Congress in the 14th District against Congressman Michael Farley, President of the National Liquor Dealers Association. Farley won in a sure district but lost 14,000 of his usual 16,000 majority.

Two years later, in 1916, before the unbelieving eyes of his own party, La Guardia defeated the unbeatable Farley. Then, because war threatened, he learned how to fly a plane before setting out for Washington.

In Congress he fought, during the early days of World War I, for civil liberties, for woman suffrage, for food control, for conscription. Then he set off for Italy where, in command of a squadron of United States flyers, he gave his superiors fits of exasperation with his indifference to official brass-hat procedures. After two years of combat service the Captain returned a Major and kept his seat in Congress by defeating the Socialist-Pacifist candidate Scott Nearing.

In the House of Representatives he fought many of Woodrow Wilson's policies but stoutly defended the League of Nations. He became the implacable foe of Volstead and his Prohibition Amendment. He introduced a resolution informing the new republics of Russia and Poland that the United States considered their persecution of the Jews within their borders a disgrace and that they could expect nothing from this country until it ceased.

He was reelected again and again. He became so popular with the polyglot population of New York that the Republican leaders yanked him, protesting excitedly, out of the House and ran him for President of the Board of Aldermen. He was elected and immediately became so busy in liberal causes that a clash with the Republican Old Guard was inevitable. When it came, La Guardia attacked the party that had put him in office as violently as ever he attacked Tammany.

Nevertheless, he expected the Republican nomination for Mayor in 1921. His wife and his little girl were dying as he campaigned for it, bitterly charging that he was being betrayed, that solemn promises were being broken. The Republican leaders refused him the nomination and named able, honest, whimsical Henry H. Curran, who was defeated by John F. Hylan.

Both major parties and a considerable proportion of the press rejoiced that the firebrand radical was now politically dead. He came alive immediately and so vigorously as an independent Republican that the party could not refuse him nomination to Congress from the 20th District. When the Tammany nominee (of Jewish blood) accused him of being anti-Semitic he sent out postcards printed in Yiddish, demanding that his opponent (who was unacquainted with the language of his ancestors) meet him in a debate to be conducted entirely in Yiddish.

He was elected and continued his independent career in Congress, laying about him vigorously, regardless of party lines. He fought Prohibition, the Ku Klux Klan, the Mellon tax bill. When horrified Republicans objected to his attacks on the national administration, he went back to Harlem to make his annual report to his constituency.

"I would rather be right than regular," he said.

Then he helped found and organize the Progressive Party. When the organization lost its power, he took over the Republican control in his district without a fight and finally in 1929 wrung the nomination for Mayor from a reluctant Republican leadership. He was soundly trounced in the election by Mayor Walker, then pathetically confident in his indifference to La Guardia's charges of corruption in city government.

La Guardia's temperament permitted no biding of time. He went back to Congress for his seventh term, with the disappointment of his failure of election to the mayoralty burning within him. Bitterly he attacked the hypocrisies of prohibition. The opponents of copyright reform received a tongue-lashing that endeared him to all creative artists. With honesty that would cost him many votes he opposed the veterans' bonus. A national sales tax bill that seemed sure of passage was defeated through his efforts. He denounced Wall Street bankers for offering bribes to writers on finance, flayed the writers for accepting the bribes. He aided the late Senator George W. Norris of Nebraska in the passage of a measure that outlawed "yellow dog contracts," (these prohibited employees from joining unions outside the company that employed them) and remedied the abuses of anti-labor injunctions.

The Democratic landslide that swept Roosevelt into the Presidency and Herbert Lehman into the governorship in 1932 swept the Republican Congressman of the 20th District

[106]

GRACIE MANSION

Wide World

into the discard. For the first time in eighteen years Tammany Hall triumphed in La Guardia's own bailiwick. Utterly discouraged, he announced his retirement from politics. "I am going to get a little place in the country and settle down and raise chickens," he said.

A week later he called an anti-Tammany mass meeting at Town Hall.

Returning to Washington for the remaining three months of his term, the "lame duck" Congressman who had just proclaimed, "They got me at last. I am too old to start over and they have wrecked my political career," found himself the choice of Franklin D. Roosevelt to sponsor New Deal legislation which the President-elect felt should be adopted even before he took office. La Guardia worked at his new duties with diligence. Then he left Congress for his retirement and

[107]

rented a cottage in Westport, Connecticut. From this vantage point he viewed the growing split between the Tammany forces for O'Brien and Edward J. Flynn's Bronx machine backing McKee. Here was an opportunity for a minority candidate to win, and no one has ever been more alive to opportunity. First he suggested a Fusion anti-Tammany ticket in a statement in which he named for the mayoralty ex-Governor Alfred E. Smith. The candidates he suggested for other offices included Robert Moses, Republican, Norman Thomas, Socialist, ex-Mayor Hylan, and Mayor O'Brien (for his old post as Surrogate). If Smith would not run, La Guardia said, he would himself. Neither Smith nor O'Brien (Tammany candidate to succeed himself) could possibly accept Fusion nomination and La Guardia knew it.

As the Republicans tried to head him off, first with Robert Moses, then with Major-General John F. O'Ryan, La Guardia played his trump card—the support of Judge Samuel Seabury whose masterful investigation of corruption in the city government had made him the hero of all friends of honesty and integrity in public affairs. Again the Republicans found themselves in the familiar position of nominating La Guardia against their inclinations. They did it, and as ever he fought every inch of the way. And this time, though Joseph McKee gave him tough opposition, he won. He was Mayor of the City of Greater New York.

In his three successive four-year terms, while the Tammany Tiger starved, Fiorello LaGuardia was the nation's busiest citizen. He was criticized for ridiculous inconsistency, for vulgar overstatement, for political opportunism. He might have hotly denied these charges, but there were moments of reflection when he knew them to be true. "When I make a mistake," he said during his third term, "it's a beaut."

His friends were more aware of his faults than his enemies were. The members of his official family at City Hall reported him confidentially as a testy tyrant, sure that he was right and that those who disagreed were for no good reason handicapping a righteous cause. His enemies admitted that he had integrity and that he was trying to give the city honest, efficient, and economical government. They had to content themselves with violent attacks on his errors and though, as he admitted, these were egregious, they were infrequent.

From the beginning to the end of his service to the city, Fiorello La Guardia fought its crooks and gamblers. He made Lewis J. Valentine, a career policeman and unpopular with Tammany, his Police Commissioner and told him to go after gangsters, racketeers, dishonest politicians, and grafting officers on his own force. Never able patiently to await the results of delegated authority, he could not help spurring Valentine with suggestions and with public denunciations of lawbreakers who should be "mussed up" or harried out of town by arrests on sight. He hated thugs and habitual criminals so much that, usually an ardent advocate of civil liberties, he intimated to a committee protesting police use of "third-degree" methods that the time to adopt regulations affecting such practices would be after he was no longer Mayor and unable to see to it that the methods were used with wisdom and discretion. Nevertheless, he brought honor and dignity back to the Police Department, which gradually became one of the finest municipal police services in the world.

The city, as a result of previous malpractices, was in an almost hopeless financial plight. By non-partisan appointments of able executives and by vigorous personal effort, La Guardia brought it to a sound financial level and kept it there. He demanded a businesslike streamlining of the governmental structure and through charter revision and county government reforms, including the abolishing of many useless jobs and the revision (to avoid political pressures) of city buying, he got it. If the town could furnish no one sufficiently experienced and able to perform important duties, he appointed men of national reputations and persuaded them to come to New York. With amazing rapidity, after his appointees went to work, the city became a safer, healthier, and happier place to live.

But efficient administration of all existing departments was not enough for the fussy, excited, nervously active little man. He had creative vision and he had dreamed of a city of such beauty and happy living as few had ever imagined. He made the best appointment of his career in selecting Robert Moses as Park Commissioner. In the years that followed, while the Commissioner and the Mayor shouted at each other in ardent disagreement and then made up, the ugly approaches to the great town that lay between the rivers and the sea became tree-lined drives affording vistas of flowing waters, high palisades, picturesque islands, sky-piercing office buildings. New parks, green in summer, filled with elderly checker-players, young mothers pushing baby carriages, racing children. New playgrounds were crowded with eager young athletes. A tremendous airport was established on the meadows of Flushing. New sand beaches near the city welcomed millions to convenient parking, good food, sanitary conveniences, clean grounds, safe swimming.

To make New York a city in which neighbors get along well together the Mayor devoted his tremendous energies to slum clearance and low-rent housing, to the settling of labor disputes, to personal investigation of even minor complaints by individual residents.

When the subway fare had been set at five cents in the administration of Mayor Gaynor, no one could have predicted the decline in buying value of the American nickel. As it lessened, succeeding mayors were plagued by the fact that the subways were losing money. Raising the fare would work hardship on the masses of people of low income, and a corollary of that fact was that such action would result in loss of support from a tremendous number of voters. From political motives and because they were genuinely friendly to working men and women, Mayors Walker and La Guardia had opposed increasing the price of a ride. The latter realized, however, that the first step toward any common-sense solution of the subway problem was for the city to obtain ownership. Though he met with bitter opposition, he succeeded in achieving city purchase of more transit lines, thus unwittingly aiding his successor's bold winning fight to raise the fare.

From the first omens of coming war, La Guardia was belligerently on the side of the democracies, denouncing fascism and nazism and their leaders with sneering contempt. Many thought him overactive in his campaign to prepare the city for possible bombing, but he kept at it, insisting on careful organization and demanding perfection in black-out techniques. He tried his best to obtain an appointment to the armed forces or to war service as an administrator in an occupied nation, but high national authorities claimed that the job he was doing for the country's largest and most important city made him too valuable to be spared.

In the twelve years he served the city as mayor he was having more fun than most men can pack into the whole of their allotted span, and the people of the city were getting almost equal enjoyment out of watching a man with a real talent for living have the time of his life. He raced to fires, and a high helmet took the place of the Stetson. He stood before great orchestras

THE FIRE DEPARTMENT IN ACTION

and waved a baton expertly. During a strike when newspapers were not delivered he read the Sunday morning comic supplements to the children of the city over the radio, and his high voice and amused chuckles made "the funnies" funnier than they had been on the printed page.

When in the summer of 1945 Fiorello La Guardia said over the radio that he would not run for reelection, few of his hearers would take him at his word. Some suspected that his announcement was a political ruse. Others believed he was resigning because of his failure to obtain an important national appointment. Still others thought he was expecting such an appointment. All were agreed that after twelve years of his uniquely active administration it would be hard to imagine the great city without him at its head.

[112]

He could not leave office without a characteristic last gesture that proved him far from politically dead. Tammany and the American Labor Party had nominated to succeed him the experienced and capable Brooklyn attorney, William O'Dwyer, whom La Guardia had defeated in the last mayoralty campaign. The Republicans, advised by Governor Dewey, had named Jonah J. Goldstein, an honest and honored judge, hoping that his fine record and the fact that he was a Jew who could depend on receiving a large proportion of the Jewish vote (30 percent of the city total) would bring about his election. La Guardia had proposed the names of a number of distinguished men, some of them Republicans, whom he would gladly support, and he resented the selection of Goldstein, who had been a Democrat until informed that he would be nominated as the Republican candidate.

With La Guardia to resent was to act. Suddenly a new party, the No-Deal Party, appeared on the New York scene, with Newbold Morris, President of the City Council, as its candidate for mayor. Morris, whose character and capabilities were unquestionable and whose connection with one of the city's oldest and most prominent families made him a sentimental choice of the town's aristocrats, was enthusiastically supported by La Guardia, whose political acumen undoubtedly told him that his candidate could not be elected and that, by splitting the Republican vote, he was immeasurably aiding the campaign of O'Dwyer. At the end of forty years of bitter warfare against Tammany, its most implacable foe was making sure that the Tiger's candidate would be elected!

O'Dwyer won the greatest plurality in the history of the city, and the man who had defeated him four years before did not seem unhappy. No one could know William O'Dwyer without believing him honest and difficult to deceive. La Guardia had never believed that a man's political party mattered much when compared with those attributes. His beloved city was in safe hands and he had much to look back upon with pride. He had been a record-breaker—the only reform mayor of the City of Greater New York ever to be reelected, the only mayor of any party to serve three consecutive terms.

Immediately on an office door in Rockefeller City, mid-town Manhattan, appeared a sign: "F. H. La Guardia—Thinking, Writing, and Talking," and, as immediately, the door was locked as the lessee took over the job of head of the United Nations Relief and Rehabilitation Administration from former Governor Lehman, who was retiring for considerations of health. Again the little man was everywhere—in Washington, in every grain-producing state, in Europe. He talked United Nations Relief with Stalin, Tito, and the Pope. He demanded a food fund of $400 million to be administered by the United Nations.

When he did not get the money, he resigned and went back to the office where the sign told what was going on inside. He wrote a column for an afternoon newspaper with all of his accustomed vigor. For a smart furniture store which paid him for the use of them in its advertisements, he wrote stinging editorials against the things he hated. *Liberty Magazine* hired him to broadcast his opinions on national affairs and then, embarrassed by his characteristic forthrightness and his passionate utterances, fired him because of what the magazine chose to call "reckless and irresponsible statements." He sold milk over the radio by stating his point of view on city affairs. Then the strong body he had developed in his boyhood under Arizona suns began to fail him. For a few months he fought as bravely as ever, knowing that he was dying. On September 20, 1947, he died in his sleep. The world mourned.

Wide World

The story of William O'Dwyer is one that happens often enough to cause Americans to think it reasonably typical and to be proud of it. The British had their Dick Whittington who was poor and became Lord Mayor of London, but Dick was, of course, and very properly too, as his countrymen would agree, every inch an Englishman. Bill O'Dwyer was poor and an alien, and Americans are inclined proudly to emphasize both those facts when they tell how he became Mayor of the largest and richest metropolis in the United States.

William O'Dwyer was twenty years old and his pockets held only $23.35 on the day in 1910 when he first saw the Statue of Liberty. His parents, Patrick and Bridget, were schoolteachers of modest means in Bohola, Mayo County, Ireland, where they reared a family of eleven children.

From his intellectual parents William inherited the inquiring mind that led him to adventuring in far places and to philosophizing as he went. When a boy, he ran away from County Mayo and sailed to Spain where he studied for two years in the Jesuit University of Salamanca because he wanted to be a priest. Like one of his remarkable predecessors in the mayor's chair, William J. Gaynor, he decided before he was twenty against the priesthood and came to New York to carve out a future. The carving during the first few years was hard. He was handyman in a Bronx grocery at $9 a week, deckhand on a freighter plying between United States and South American ports, stoker and later fireman on a Hudson River steamboat, a plasterer's apprentice, and he once presided for a while with the required combination of skill, dignity, and bonhomie behind a bar of the Hotel Plaza.

He became a citizen of his new country in 1916 and as soon as possible thereafter he married Catherine Lenihan, former telephone operator at the Hotel Vanderbilt, a witty, wise, and understanding woman usually described by the Mayor's biographers, without meaning to include the stuffiness usually associated with the term, as a "good influence."

About a year after William O'Dwyer became a citizen and a benedict, he became a New York policeman. Urged on by the "good influence" he studied law in night school while enforcing it in the daytime, and in six years held a diploma from Fordham Law School. By 1926 he had resigned from the police force and had his own law practice. And when Joseph V. McKee was Acting-Mayor in December, 1932, William O'Dwyer received his first political appointment, that of City Magistrate.

Five years later, to fill a vacancy, Governor Lehman made the rising attorney a Judge of the County Court in Brooklyn, and the next year he was elected to a full term of fourteen years. He risked the honors and financial security that go with this office when in the following year he stepped down from the bench to run for District Attorney of Brooklyn.

O'Dwyer's record as District Attorney was so outstanding that it led to many greater honors. The criminal world had become so powerful in Brooklyn that a gang, dubbed by the press Murder, Incorporated, had made a profitable business out of murder for hire. The District Attorney prosecuted these men fearlessly and efficiently, obtaining many convictions. During his two terms he was reported to have solved no less than eighty-seven murders. He had been in office only two years, however, when he ran against La Guardia for the mayoralty and was defeated. At the end of the same year war came, and he wired President Roosevelt an offer of his services. First appointed as a Major in the Provost Marshal's office in New York, he ended his brilliant war services to the national government as a Brigadier General, chief of the Allied Control Commission in Italy, and personal representative of the President with the rank of Minister. While absent in war work he had run for reelection as District Attorney in a sure campaign, since he was indorsed by all major parties.

MAYOR O'DWYER RECEIVES A SALUTE

GROVER A. WHALEN REVIEWS THE PARADE

In 1945 O'Dwyer was again nominated for mayor. Tammany and the American Labor Party supported him against Judge Goldstein, the Republican nominee, and Newbold Morris, La Guardia's candidate on a No-Deal Party ticket. When offered the nomination, O'Dwyer proved his independence of Tammany by refusing to run on the Tiger ticket unless all its nominees were satisfying to him. Once this matter was arranged he campaigned so wisely and vigorously that he was overwhelmingly elected.

The O'Dwyer administration in its third year, which is the year of celebrating the 50th Anniversary of the founding of the City of Greater New York, has won wide approval and high respect. The Mayor, whose reputation for honesty and integrity was firmly established in the days when he was an "honest cop," approaches his problems with a thoughtfulness and objectivity that are a strange contrast with the impetuosity and hot personal prejudices of his predecessor. He has kept a number of La Guardia's best appointees, including that great city planner, Robert Moses, and Police Commissioner Arthur W. Wallender, successor to the retired Commissioner Valentine.

The Mayor has not been afraid to fire his own appointees when they have proved unworthy, and his replacements have been well considered. When Tammany proved critical of his efficiency and honesty he went determinedly into Tammany Hall. When he came out, Tammany was for the moment a quiet, disciplined organization which took its orders from the Mayor. This led to the bad mauling of a famous limerick about a long since devoured "young lady from Niger" by an exultant independent voter who wrote:

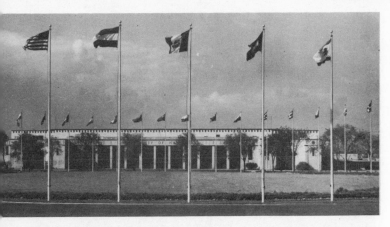

UNITED NATIONS, FLUSHING MEADOWS   *Official United Nations Photos*

THE ASSEMBLY IN SESSION   [121]

EAST RIVER SITE OF THE NEW
UNITED NATIONS HEADQUARTERS

Official United Nations

MODEL OF THE UNITED NATIONS HEADQUARTERS

A broth of a fellow from Eire
Smiled as he rode on a Tiger.
They came back from the ride
With the Tiger inside
And the smile on the face of the Mayor.

Old William J. Gaynor had fought a losing fight to "swallow the Tiger" but apparently William O'Dwyer had done it with aplomb. He was soon to discover, however, that one swallow does not slay a tiger.

The "good influence" died his first year in office, but with her help the Mayor had already plotted his course. He has attacked his work cleanly and with a philosophic calm that is greatly aided by a sense of humor. Nevertheless, he has on occasion driven himself too hard for his own health and therefore for the good of the town. He has championed New York in Albany against the inequities which a misunderstanding and mistrusting Republican up-state majority is ever inclined to force upon a city which is likely to vote Democratic and to indulge in vices which good cock-fighting, applejack-making farmers know nought of. He has established a committee on the solution of labor disputes which does its best to solve difficulties before they reach the strike stage. He has, with rare courage and disregard of political consequences, met the subway problem squarely and advocated and won a ten-cent fare— this in the face of opposition of some unions and the slurs of caviling critics who accuse him of raising the fares in order to increase the Tammany graft that is bound to come. In a period when civil rights are threatened, he has opposed legislation which would endanger them. He worked long and hard to bring the capitol of the United Nations to New York.

In La Guardia's three terms and the first three years of Mayor

O'Dwyer the City of Greater New York has had fifteen years of upright and intelligent government. It has become used to this and is not likely to accept any other kind without complaint. America's greatest city enters the second half of its first century proud of the past symbolized by its monuments and the beauty of its relics of another day, proud of its present filled with great buildings and alive with a sense of magnificent achievement, proud of the future it may expect as a center to which all nations may look for the light that may bring lasting peace to the world.

The City's Business

By THOMAS C. COCHRAN

SUPERLATIVES come easily in speaking of the economic life of New York: the world's richest city, largest port, and most populous metropolitan area. But, in many ways, such phrases fail to state the true importance of the five boroughs. Since the early nineteenth century, forces not shown in census tables have bestowed upon the city a position unique in the life of the nation. Because of its greatness as a center of imports, the banks of the nation kept reserve deposits in New York. Because of this accumulation of funds New York became the security trading center. This in turn drew still more capitalists, and their wealth made New York the center for marketing securities. Gradually New Yorkers came to own or control enterprises all over the country, and many entrepreneurs left their local factories to resident managers and established head offices on Manhattan Island.

By the turn of the century, business and financial leadership had already migrated to New York. Its position as the nation's financial center was undisputed. Of the 185 largest industrial combinations in the nation, 69, controlling 2,416 plants, had their head offices in the metropolis. The port received nearly two-thirds of the nation's imports, by value, and shipped about 40 percent of the total exports. More

GANSEVOORT MARKET, LITTLE WEST 12TH STREET

than two-thirds of all the immigrants from Europe came through the Federal inspection station at Ellis Island, to provide poorly paid but ambitious workers for the city's industries.

Why had such a concentration of economic and social power arisen in a broad continental nation with many other seaports? The basic factor was the superiority of the Port of New York. Deep water on both sides of Manhattan Island and along the protected shores of Brooklyn, Staten Island, and Jersey provide 771 miles of frontage for docks adjacent to railroads, factories, and markets. Estuaries and fine natural basins, such as the East River, Newark Bay, and the smaller inlets of Brooklyn and Queens, open great areas to direct water transportation. Ice never seriously impedes winter operations, and severe fogs are rarer than in most North Atlantic ports. A broad channel leads in from the ocean to the harbor mouth, and no formidable barriers must be skirted in gaining entrance. As a consequence New York not only became the favorite port of foreign shippers but also the natural point for the transfer of South Atlantic and Gulf Coast products to trans-Atlantic vessels.

In addition to immediate facilities superior to those of other American ports, New York opened upon an imperial hinterland. The earliest steamboats made the Raritan River a highway to central Jersey, Long Island Sound the gateway to southern New England, and the Hudson River, and later the Erie Canal, the best route to the West. By the time

5TH AVENUE AT 44TH STREET, 1898

railroads brought Western connections to Boston or Philadelphia, New York had gained an irresistible momentum that, snowball-like, added to her economic superiority decade after decade. The port itself is, therefore, the logical point of departure for an account of the economic progress of the Greater City.

South Street was the center of the American shipping world in 1898. Shipowners still liked to live on Brooklyn Heights in houses from which they could see their vessels. Australian, Far Eastern, and California products still came around the Horn by sail, and the tall masts and long spars of these big cargo carriers towered above the steamers. Smaller coastwise sailing vessels added to the forest of masts and rigging. But during the next decade maritime progress eliminated most of these reminders of the great days of sail. As the West Coast boomed, the American-Hawaiian Steamship Company built the biggest fleet of steel cargo steamers under the American flag to carry the products of Hawaii and the coast, around the Horn until 1907, then by rail shuttle across the Isthmus of Tehuantepec, and finally through the Panama Canal. Meanwhile, small steamers replaced the heterogeneous sailing craft of the coastwise trade, and sail became rarer on British tramps. By 1910 the South Street forest of furled sails had almost disappeared, leaving only the bare masts and low funnels of steamers.

Freight and passenger services, although often combined on the same ship, present essentially different problems. As the chief business, recreation, and job-providing center, New York was reasonably sure of attracting human cargoes, but freight bound in or out of the interior would go by way of the port that offered the best service at the lowest cost. The Mississippi Valley was farther by rail from New York than from Baltimore or Philadelphia, and smaller ports could provide as good or better facilities for handling certain bulk commodities. Consequently the history of the Port of New York in the twentieth century has involved a continual effort by the city to hold its position in sea-borne trade by improved facilities—to overcome the "curse of bigness" in handling freight.

Between 1902 and 1907, the city invested $15,000,000 in building nine large North River piers which it rented to steamship companies. But in spite of this and other lesser expenditures for improvements, New York from 1898 to 1914 failed to hold its relative position in American trade. In 1899 about 37 percent of American exports and 67 percent of imports, by value, passed through the port. By 1913, the last year unaffected by war, the export percentage re-

THE FREE PORT, STATEN ISLAND

A WAR SHIPMENT TO FRANCE, 1940   *The Staten Island Advance*

mained the same, but imports, because of the rise of Southern
and Western ports, had dropped to 58 percent of the national
total.

The first World War raised problems more serious than
the matter of relative progress. The facilities of the port
proved in many ways inadequate to handle the threefold
increase in exports between 1914 and 1918. Railroad yards
and pier facilities were overcrowded. At the worst, in February of 1918, over 200,000 freight cars were tied up waiting
their turn for unloading, while interior points lacked cars to
move essential war materials. The crisis produced momentous
results. The President exercised his previously granted power
to take control of the railroads. By making the best use of all
available terminals without regard to ownership, the railroad

congestion was gradually reduced. Starting in 1917, the Federal Government developed Port Newark, and the President appointed for the Port a War Board with Irving Bush (whose name is borne by the great Bush Terminal in Brooklyn, a huge docking and storage development) as executive officer. But long-run improvement was largely a problem of securing the cooperation of the states of New Jersey and New York.

Luckily, both states had able, vigorous governors. Walter E. Edge of New Jersey and Charles S. Whitman of New York appointed a joint Harbor Development Commission

PORT AUTHORITY GRAIN TERMINAL

to plan works that neither state could undertake alone. While few new facilities could be added quickly enough to help defeat Germany, the Commission did not forget the lessons of the war. In 1920 they issued a report based on a careful study of railroad, truck, and water-borne operations. They called for terminal markets, a foreign trade zone, a bridge across the Hudson, and vehicular tunnels. Alfred E. Smith, who had succeeded Whitman as Governor of New York, endorsed the report enthusiastically and set to work to secure action. He urged on the people and the legislature the need "to make some changes in the old-fashioned, worn-out, dilapidated ways of doing business in this port." The Governor's wishes prevailed, and the state legislature set about the complicated procedures necessary to erect an interstate authority. First a treaty was drawn up between the "sovereign" states of New York and New Jersey, and in 1921, to insure legality, the compact was approved by Act of Congress. Under the sanction of the treaty a Port of New York Authority was established. The Authority is a self-supporting, non-political, regional agency that has established a reputation for efficient conduct of business. By issuing its own bonds, plus a little stock, it has financed some $250 million worth of improvements in the port, including a union terminal for eight trunk-line railroads, a union motor truck terminal, and six tunnels and bridges connecting Manhattan and Richmond with New Jersey. In order to save shippers the time and expense of customs inspection and bonding for goods intended for reexport, it opened in 1937 a duty free Foreign Trade Zone on Staten Island for the deposit and transshipment of foreign goods. The Authority has been able at all times to meet its obligations from revenues in rents and tolls.

WAR SHIPMENTS TO ENGLAND AND RUSSIA, *Brown Brothers*
STATEN ISLAND

Other port developments are of great importance. Private interests have helped build the Brooklyn Eastern District Terminal into one of the chief warehousing and freight transfer centers of the country. The New York Dock Company Terminal, also in Brooklyn, comprises an impressive set of facilities. Mayor Hylan built thirteen piers along the Stapleton waterfront at a cost of thirty millions, and though they were long called "Hylan's Folly," in World War II they proved decidedly useful.

Up to 1929, partly because of the work of the Port Authority, New York held to her pre-war share of the national export trade. The drop in imports through New York to a

[133]

little under 50 percent of the national dollar total was due largely to greater overland trade from Canada, as well as Latin American shipments to more southerly ports. The city also maintained its old leadership in the coastwise and inter-coastal trades. The depression struck a severe blow at foreign trade and consequently at the prosperity of the port, but compared with the trade of the country as a whole New York retained about her same position. With the outbreak of war in 1939, however, shipments to Europe began to mount and by 1940 New York's share of exports had risen to an unprecedented 48 percent. As long as government lending and European Recovery Plans boom European trade, the port will have unusual prosperity.

Nothing in the fifty years since 1898 has threatened the city's near-monopoly of fast transatlantic passenger travel. From the 17,274-ton *Oceanic* of 1899 to the 85,000-ton *Queen Elizabeth* of 1940 each new giant liner has raced to an elaborate welcome in New York. Transatlantic planes lack the majesty and glamor of great steamships, but they are continuing the pattern of delivering passengers from abroad at New York. In some future day, flights across the polar wastes may terminate at Chicago or Detroit, but so far New York remains secure as the gateway to the continent.

The efficiency of operation of the port in World War II contrasts pleasantly with its near-breakdown in World War I. Military shipments to Europe again brought unusual trade to New York: in 1939 this was 48.7 percent of American trade by volume; in 1944, despite the rise of Far Eastern shipments from Pacific ports, it was 53.5 percent. In coastwise trade the gain was from 42.4 percent for 1939 to 49.4 percent for 1944. In the latter year stevedores, often working day and night, stowed 21,000,000 tons, more than double the

[134]

peacetime load, on vessels bound abroad. Through the long-range planning of transportation companies and the Port Authority, freight cars and trucks were kept moving and ships were loaded as rapidly as in smaller ports.

Although foreign and coastwise shipping originally gave New York its greatness and its unique character among American cities, the sea has been a relatively small part of the transportation system. Not only goods for export, but vast quantities of raw materials consumed by the city itself reach the area by rail or truck. In 1900 the railroad had scarcely been challenged by any other carrier of overland freight. Eight trunk-line railroads, connecting with all parts of the continent, converged on New York. The Pennsylvania, the Central Railroad of New Jersey, the Philadelphia and Reading, the Baltimore and Ohio, and the Lehigh Valley reached the North River at Jersey City over routes running south of the Watchung mountains. Several branches of the Delaware, Lackawanna and Western, and the Erie wound through the hills of northern Jersey to terminals at Hoboken and Jersey City; the West Shore, controlled by the New York Central, clung to narrow cuts down the precipitous west bank of the Hudson to reach its terminal at West New York. The four-track New York Central main line, winding in sweeping curves along the east bank of the river, forked at Spuyten Duyvil, one branch taking freight down the west shore of Manhattan, the other turning southeast to join the New York, New Haven and Hartford tracks ending at Grand Central Terminal. In 1898 these two lines, plus the Long Island Railroad (terminating at Long Island City in Queens) and the Baltimore and Ohio's Staten Island Rapid Transit Railroad, serving Richmond, were the only roads operating within the city limits.

GRAND CENTRAL TERMINAL IN THE
RAILROAD STRIKE, 1946

Wide World

The manner of distributing rail-borne freight from the
terminals of Jersey, the Bronx, Queens, and Brooklyn has
not changed since 1898. While only the New York Central
had yards on Manhattan Island, this and other roads delivered loaded freight cars by ferries to all parts of the harbor.
Since these transfers were included in the through rates,
water transit between through train and factory siding did
not add significantly to total transportation cost, but for deliveries on Manhattan Island, where cars must be unloaded
at North River piers, the system has tied up a great deal of
valuable dock space.

The leisurely pace of distribution by car-ferry was no great
disadvantage in the case of freight, but changing to boats

[136]

was irksome to busy passengers. For thirty years, prior to 1899, the Pennsylvania system had been considering ways of entering Manhattan Island from the west, but no solution had seemed practical. At this juncture the Pennsylvania elected a new President, Alexander J. Cassatt, a civil engineer who had risen to be First Vice-President in 1880, only to retire two years later, at the age of forty-three, to be a gentleman farmer. When recalled to leadership he had fresh ideas about almost everything connected with railroad operation. In 1900 he persuaded his Board to buy a controlling interest in the Long Island Railroad. Studying the extension of the Orléans railway into Paris, in 1901, he became convinced of the practicality of electrified lines passing under rivers. Cassatt at once applied his ideas to Manhattan Island. In this same year he started to acquire the necessary mid-town land. On October 9, 1902, he secured the franchise from the city, on January 10, 1903, he ordered work begun on the North River tunnel and, on May 1, 1904, on the Seventh Avenue passenger terminal. In addition he started tunneling under the East River to connect with the Long Island Railroad. Desiring a monument to the greatness of the Pennsylvania system, he commissioned the New York firm of McKim, Mead and White, famous for their classic buildings, including the main group at the Chicago World's Fair, to design the enormous station. Cassatt barely lived to see the North River tunnel completed late in 1906. The station was not opened for regular train service until 1910. His farsighted plans reached their logical conclusion in 1917 when the New York Connecting Railroad, jointly owned by the New York, New Haven and Hartford and the Pennsylvania, bridged the mouth of Long Island Sound at Hell Gate, making it possible to ship freight from Long

HELL GATE RAILROAD BRIDGE   *Brown Brothers*

Island factory sidings directly to New England, and for passenger trains to run from Boston to Washington.

In 1903 the New York Central also decided to electrify its lines and erect a new terminal building. William J. Wilgus planned the operating system, and the firm of Warren and Wetmore designed the Renaissance station. Although the building was not completed until 1913, by 1907 most of the trains were running into Manhattan under electric power. The addition of a second level of tracks in 1927 made Grand Central unique among American terminals.

In the eighteen seventies a New York, Westchester, and Boston railroad had been planned as a blackmail line against the New Haven. Although many of the original investors did not live to see success, the plan ultimately worked. The promoters had acquired some property for the right-of-way but had laid no tracks, when in 1906 a New York, New Haven, and Hartford committee, headed by J. Pierpont Morgan and William Rockefeller, the brother of John D., Sr., believing that their company should control all competition, bought the property. The price was $11,000,000. Construction of the road by the New Haven added $25,000,000 more, or a total of $36,000,000 for eighteen miles of first-line track between the Harlem River at 133d Street and various points in Westchester. Running in close competition with the commuting services of the New Haven main line and the New York Central, both of which went direct to Grand Central, the new company never made money. In 1937 the courts permitted the receivers to abandon service and dispose of the property. The tracks remain unused, a monument to one of the world's greatest railroad follies, but also a basis for some future express highway.

While the steamship and railroad had largely solved the problem of bringing passengers and goods in and out of New York and other metropolitan areas, no city had dealt satisfactorily with internal transportation. Cable cars and horse cars moved people to and from work at a snail's pace. Business in the central part of the city was strangled by the congestion of surface cars and horse-drawn trucks. Except for the Brooklyn Bridge, opened in 1883, all movement between Long Island, Manhattan, and New Jersey was by ferry.

The first steps in the direction of rapid transit were the elevated lines built in the late sixties and seventies, but as long as they were steam-powered they were far from an ideal solution to the movement of urban passengers. Electrification of the trolley and "El" lines from 1899 on helped greatly to eliminate smoke and increase speed, but, most important of all, electricity brought subways.

The Board of Rapid Transit Commissioners had been considering a Manhattan-Bronx subway since their appointment in 1894, but the adverse pressure of the existing private transportation companies and other political delays prevented action until 1900. In the final plan the city was to pay for the construction and lease the property for fifty years to a private operating company. The veteran railroad construction man John B. McDonald, famed for his Baltimore and Ohio railroad tunnel under Baltimore, won the contract for $35,000,000, and financier August Belmont joined with him in setting up the Interborough Rapid Transit Company. Construction on the East-Side line was begun March 24, 1900, and by 1904 the line was opened from Brooklyn Bridge to West Farms in the Bronx.

During the next thirty-five years there was almost always a new subway under construction in some part of the city. In 1907 the lines reached Brooklyn, in the next decade for a new operating company—the Brooklyn-Manhattan Transit Corporation—the city built connections over and under the East River, and in the thirties the municipally run Independent System built lines the length of Manhattan Island and into Brooklyn, the Bronx, and Queens. In 1940, the city, led by energetic Mayor La Guardia, took over the leases and other assets of the IRT and BMT in return for $326,-000,000 in municipal bonds. By this time the outer fringes of all the boroughs except Richmond were connected with each other and with Manhattan by elevated and subway. Meanwhile, in 1908, the privately financed Hudson and Manhattan Railroad Company tunneled the North River and connected Newark, Jersey City, and Hoboken with Manhattan.

New York's bridges are older and more numerous than its underwater tunnels. By 1898 there were many bridges over the Harlem River between Manhattan and the Bronx, while only the Brooklyn Bridge connected Manhattan and Long Island. In the first decade of the new century the East River was spanned by the Williamsburg Bridge in 1903, and by both the Manhattan and the Queensborough in 1909. Bridging the Hudson and the Sound was more difficult because of the length of span and height required, and vehicular bridges over the Kill Van Kull and Arthur Kill between

HENRY HUDSON BRIDGE

Triborough Bridge and Tunnel Authority

TRIBOROUGH BRIDGE: BRONX CROSSING
AND HARLEM RIVER LIFT SPAN

New York City Department of Parks

Richmond and New Jersey were less urgent. These enterprises were undertaken in the late twenties and thirties under the planning and direction of Othmar H. Ammann, chief engineer for bridges for New York City and also for the Triborough Bridge and Port of New York Authorities. The George Washington Bridge over the Hudson at 180th Street, designed by architect Cass Gilbert and completed by the Port Authority in 1931, had for a time the longest suspended span in the world (3,500 feet) and remains the city's most impressive bridge. The Triborough Bridge Authority, established in 1933 as an independent self-supporting business corporation after the model of the Port Authority, completed the four-span Triborough Bridge connecting the Bronx, Manhattan, and Queens in 1937, and the uniquely beautiful Bronx-Whitestone Bridge farther up the Sound in 1939.

Meanwhile, Robert Moses, Chairman of the Triborough Authority and Commissioner of Parks in charge of parkway development, was in a position to create a coordinated system for motor transportation. With strong backing from Mayor La Guardia he made rapid progress. Under his direction in the nineteen thirties four-lane superhighways were built along the east and west sides of Manhattan and through the other boroughs. Continuing the policy of building major bridges by independent corporations with bonded indebtedness serviced from tolls, Mr. Moses became the sole commissioner of the Henry Hudson Parkway Authority, which completed in 1936 the two-deck Henry Hudson Bridge at the northern tip of Manhattan. In 1938 this Authority and a Marine Parkway Authority, that had been bridging parts of Jamaica Bay in southern Queens and Brooklyn, were combined into the New York City Parkway Authority.

The Holland Tunnel, used more than any other approach

GRAND CENTRAL PARKWAY, QUEENS

to New York, was commenced by New York State and New Jersey at the end of the first World War to connect Jersey City with lower Manhattan. Completed in 1927, the tunnel was turned over to the Port Authority in 1930. Seven years later the Authority completed the south tube of the Lincoln Tunnel to mid-town Manhattan. The Queens-Midtown Tunnel to Long Island City, opened in 1940, and the war-delayed Brooklyn-Battery tunnel, to be opened in 1949, both controlled by the Triborough Bridge and Tunnel Authority, will temporarily complete the unique and costly series of roadways under and over the waters of the port.

As a result of these expenditures, New York has kept entrance and exit facilities abreast of the rapid increase in automobiles; for light vehicles, permitted on the parkways, travel is quicker than in most cities of one-tenth its size. There is almost no long trip between the boroughs that cannot be made, for most of the distance, by express highway. The replacement of streetcars by buses, from the twenties on, also has helped to speed up local surface transportation, but overcrowded streets in lower Manhattan remain the most serious economic problem of the regional transportation system. The relatively narrow cross streets of the early nineteenth century gridiron plan were not designed for unloading trailer trucks. The war and post-war boom of the nineteen forties has consequently presented the city with another challenge to overcome the "curse of bigness."

Air transport was of minor importance during most of this last half-century. Although there were some half-dozen airports near by, including New York City's Floyd Bennett Field (opened in 1931), Newark Airport, a pioneer of the twenties, continued to receive most of the traffic up to the completion of North Beach Airport (called La Guardia

[144]

HARLEM RIVER SPEEDWAY

The Port of New York Authority
Triborough Bridge and Tunnel Authority

QUEENS MIDTOWN TUNNEL

Field) in 1939. During and after the war, air traffic increased so fast that La Guardia and Newark, combined, became inadequate for the load. The opening in 1948 of New York International Airport Anderson Field at Idlewild, Queens, a much bigger airport on Jamaica Bay, again readjusted the traffic between the major fields of the port. To facilitate such adjustment and avoid interstate rivalries the Port Authority, on June 1, 1947, took over the lease of both La Guardia and International.

The purpose of most of the passenger travel in and out of New York is trade in the country's greatest wholesale and retail market. Between one and two hundred thousand mer-

The Port of New York Authority

WATCHING OPERATIONS AT LA GUARDIA AIRPORT

chants or buying representatives annually visit the clothing market alone. Over most of the last fifty years more of the city's people have been employed in trade than in any other activity. Long before the turn of the century New York had established itself as the chief wholesale market for clothing, jewelry, furs, and imported goods ranging from French perfumes to tea or coffee. About half the dollar volume of the trade in domestic and imported commodities has been in food, drygoods, and clothing. In spite of the growth of interior markets, New York has continued to retain its leadership. In fact, its percentage of the value of United States wholesale trade increased from 22.8 percent in 1929 to 23.4 percent in 1939.

All types of agents, brokers, jobbers, buyers, assemblers, and warehousemen make up the wholesale traders of New York. In 1939 there were 15,827 separate firms operating 24,-042 establishments and employing 241,405 men. Among these were nearly 500 resident buyers' offices serving over 10,000 out-of-town stores. About one man in six in the wholesale trade of the United States worked in New York City. Some worked in mahogany-paneled office buildings and dealt on exchanges, others in open fruit and vegetable markets dealing with farmers, local grocers, and on occasion with racketeers.

About 90 percent of the trade has been done in locations that during the twentieth century have changed only slightly. The leather market is on the East Side, south of the Brooklyn Bridge, in what used to be called the "Swamp"; the wholesale food sellers still line the lower water fronts near the piers and the Holland Tunnel; and the furriers have remained just above 23d Street. Wholesalers who wish to be near the fashionable retail outlets have moved uptown but chiefly below 59th Street.

A large part of the retail trade is carried on in more than 100,000 neighborhood stores, with some 350,000 employees scattered throughout the boroughs. Supplying almost every type of commodity to every section of the city, these differ little from similar stores in other centers throughout the United States. But the great Manhattan retail district of department stores and specialty shops was peculiar to New York even in 1900, and has never been equaled elsewhere. Regent Street or Rue Madeleine at the turn of the century may have had a few more famous shops, but neither London nor Paris had such a concentration of department stores as could be found in Manhattan between 14th and 23d Streets. In addition another group of large department stores was developing in downtown Brooklyn.

The Straus family, who owned Macy's, were responsible for the first important desertion of the nineteenth century Manhattan area. By 1900 the old Macy store on 14th Street at Sixth Avenue, composed of a conglomeration of old buildings opening into each other, needed so many repairs and improvements that the partners decided to take the risk of moving uptown. Jesse and Percy, Isidore's sons, were given the task of finding a new location. In selecting 34th Street and Broadway, ten blocks above the northern boundary of the then fashionable shopping region, they did even better than they could have guessed. The Hudson "Tubes" were already planned to terminate at 33d Street and Sixth Avenue, but the Seventh and Sixth Avenue subways and the Pennsylvania-Long Island Railroad Terminal were all unpredictable gains. This bold stroke of entrepreneurship ultimately gave Macy's the best location in the city for shoppers in the middle-income brackets.

At the outbreak of the first World War, 34th Street be-

Wide World

SHOPPING ON 5TH AVENUE

tween Seventh and Fifth avenues and northward a few blocks on Fifth was the fashionable area. What may be the final relocation began shortly after the war, when certain fashionable shops, skipping the 42d Street district, began to move up Fifth Avenue to the fifties and eastward to Madison Avenue. But as most of the older department stores remained in their former locations around 34th Street, and Wanamaker's at its original location on 9th Street, the new movement was a spreading out rather than a general migration. Since the limits of the best area are set to a considerable degree on the south, east, and west, by the position of Grand Cen-

[149]

tral and Pennsylvania stations, and on the north by Central Park, it is quite possible that the current mid-town shopping district will be permanent.

While Manhattan will probably remain the major shopping center, it is losing in relative importance to Brooklyn, Queens, the Bronx, and Richmond. The rise of the automobile in the twenties led to both an increased emigration of upper-income families and the possibility of avoiding traffic congestion by buying in suburban centers. Some of the big central Manhattan firms kept pace with this movement by establishing suburban branches, but the net result was a decline of retail trade, not only on the Island but in Greater New York as a whole, from 9 percent of the national total in 1929 to 7.6 percent in 1939. Thus the bigness of New York works both for and against its central shopping districts.

In the borderland between trade and manufacturing lie hotels and amusements. Taken together, and it is hard to separate them, they constitute one of the city's major activities. By 1929 its 509 hotels, mainly in Manhattan and Brooklyn, had 42,000 employees. The $165,000,000 in annual receipts was nearly a fifth of the national total. Theaters and other places of amusement probably had about half as many employees as the hotels, but took in at least as much money. While both businesses were hard hit by the depression, hotel receipts dropping to $61,000,000 in 1933, they recovered rapidly in World War II. But the importance of these activities to New York cannot be measured directly. Almost every type of trade benefits to some degree from the fame of New York's hotels, restaurants, theaters and night clubs.

George C. Boldt, a self-made immigrant from an island in

the Baltic Sea who leased the Waldorf-Astoria from William Waldorf Astor, was one of the chief contributors to New York's fame for lavish entertainment. He and his Swiss maître-d'hôtel Oscar Tschirky, better known as "Oscar of the Waldorf," made the thousand-room establishment in the then residential district of Fifth Avenue the national symbol of sophisticated elegance. Oscar unobtrusively educated newly rich Americans in what to eat and drink. The United States Steel Company and countless other business ventures are said to have first been conceived within the portals of the old Waldorf. Politicians, sportsmen, and foreign nobility joined the businessmen in making the hotel's Peacock Alley the most famous meeting place in early twentieth century

Wide World

52D STREET IN THE FUEL SHORTAGE

New York. Boldt died in 1916 and was succeeded as manager by Lucius M. Boomer, famed since 1912 for his success with the new Hotel McAlpin. In 1929, Boomer, as head of the Boomer-Du Pont Properties Corporation, decided to tear down the old building and move the Waldorf-Astoria to its new location at Park Avenue and Forty-ninth Street.

The "golden age" of the Waldorf coincided with the great days of the New York stage. Between 1898 and World War I, producers like the Shubert brothers, Oscar Hammerstein, John Cort, and Klaw and Erlanger steadily increased the size and number of legitimate theaters. While many companies went on the road, anyone wanting a full variety of first-class entertainment had to come to New York.

During these same years the industry that was gradually to undermine the city's dominance of the theatrical world had its beginnings in New York. Commercial moving pictures were first exhibited in America by the great rivals in the vaudeville business—F. F. Proctor and B. F. Keith. Each commenced showing pictures in their theaters in 1899, and film production quickly developed in the New York suburbs. But it was New Yorkers Fox and Loew with their neighborhood theaters, from 1906 on, who really made the movies a mass medium. The rise of the many-reel picture with pretensions, at least, to dramatic art during World War I, and of sound equipment in the late twenties, practically eliminated vaudeville and greatly diminished the importance of the legitimate stage. By the end of World War II, of New York's 668 theaters only 173 were classed as "legitimate" as against 495 moving picture theaters, and a considerable number of the legitimate houses were given over to showing first-run films. Meanwhile most of the moving picture producers had long since left New York for the better all-year-round climate of Hollywood. The radio and the phonograph also tended to decentralize entertainment. Pitted against these mechanical forces that made much the same entertainment available in Medicine Hat as in New York has been the continuing vigor of the legitimate stage and the intangible appeal of reality over the image. The post-war boom has indicated that New York's position as the entertainment center of the nation is still reasonably secure.

If one divides New York's major economic activities into manufacturing, retail trade, wholesale trade and finance, manufacturing has steadily been the most important. It has employed the most people and produced the largest gross income for the city. But, like retail trade, it has, particularly in the

TIMES SQUARE ENTERTAINS

last two decades, suffered a relative decline. Part of this has been the loss of plants to outlying parts of the metropolitan area, part from still broader decentralization of industry throughout near-by states, and part from the increasing importance of new industries in younger areas.

But plants located throughout the nation continued to retain metropolitan head offices. In 1926, of the 232 companies (including many non-manufacturing concerns) used by Standard Statistics in compiling its stock index, 70 percent had head offices in New York City. In 1942, the corresponding percentage of the firms from this group that were still in business had fallen to about 65 percent. The decline probably illustrates the reversal of the earlier trend toward moving administrative offices from plants to centers of trade and finance. But the fact that many companies that have moved away continue to sell through metropolitan dealers and finance themselves through the city banks partly explains the greater stability of New York's wholesale trade and finance.

In judging the relative status of the city in the manufacturing of the nation, the important consideration is the value added by manufacture, the actual income produced in New York. On this basis, the city's share, which had been 11 percent of the national total at the beginning of the century, declined gradually prior to 1914 and somewhat more rapidly from then until 1939, until it was only 7.5 percent. The picture is much the same with respect to wage earners employed in manufacturing establishments.

But regardless of the trend toward the suburbs and the countryside, the pattern of New York industries has remained surprisingly constant over the last fifty years. If comparisons are based on value added by manufacture, between 1899 and 1939 the same industries—clothing, printing and publishing, machine and foundry products, food products, chemicals and allied products—remained the leading five. Tobacco manufacture, formerly the sixth most important manufacturing activity in 1899, was the only major industry that virtually left New York. It was largely eliminated by the decline in cigar smoking and the trend away from Turkish tobacco, as well as by the rise of highly mechanized plants in the South.

The continuity in the statistics indicates that the factors which drew certain industries to New York in the nineteenth century have tended to keep them there in the twentieth. Good labor supply and the great wholesale and retail markets were the chief magnets; opposed to these were the lack of local raw materials, high land values, taxes and construction costs. Obviously New York City proper could not attract heavy industry with its extensive investment in plant, or industries closely tied to sources of raw materials. The clothing industry, as the figures prove, represented the ideal elements for location in New York: efficient operation in a small plant, little investment in space and equipment in relation to output, a demand for skilled and semi-skilled labor, and close relationship to stylistic and market trends.

Of the forces attracting business to New York, only the labor market has changed greatly during the last half century. Up to 1914 there was not only an abundance of high-priced skilled workers, but also the greatest national supply of low-priced immigrant labor. Dresses, for example, were made by miserably paid immigrant seamstresses working under contract in small shops or tenements. The rise of unions after 1910, further mechanization in 1910–20, and immigration restriction after 1921 all altered this situation. Dresses came to be made in factories, and New York wages came to be the highest in the nation. But the reliability and skill of New York workers,

NEW YORK LEADS IN THE CLOTHING INDUSTRY *Brown Brothers*

together with the nearness of the manufacturer to his market, has sustained the leading position of the New York dress industry and has held most of the rest of the women's clothing industry in the city.

Goods sold for out-of-city consumption are said to be for a primary market, those for home consumption for the secondary. This apparent inversion in order is because a city is far from self-sufficient and must sell goods or services to the surrounding country in order to support itself. Two of the three major industries that have grown most rapidly since 1899, baking and other food products, are mainly secondary. Essentially, their growth indicates a transference of operations from home to factory and an increase in city population. Chemicals, which grew almost as fast as these two classes of food products, are sold in both primary and secondary markets, but the increased use of cosmetics and pharmaceuticals within the city probably accounts for most of the advance. Clothing and, to a lesser degree, printed matter and machinery are the chief sources of New York's "export surplus."

New York, like other light industry centers, is a city of small factories and shops. Although the trend over the last fifty years has been toward more workers per plant, industrialists have built no giant works such as those within Pittsburgh or South Chicago. In 1899 the city had 39,776 manufacturing establishments employing an average of about 12 workers each; by 1939 the average of the 26,651 establishments had risen to 19 workers, but was still far under the average of 40 employees per plant for manufacturing establishments in the United States as a whole.

Small firms make for a highly competitive situation. The drive, thrift, and general business acumen necessary for survival in the clothing or specialty fields in New York have become proverbial. Of 1,687 dress firms reported by the New York Dress Joint Board as doing business in 1925, 83.6 percent had discontinued by 1933. New York textile-makers in particular were under continuous pressure in the twenties and thirties from the rapid rise of rayon and the ruinous competition from the South. Printers suffered similarly from cut-throat practices by their local competitors and from new presses in low-wage rural areas. Only those businessmen achieved success who combined in the right proportions advantageous location, managerial skill, and good fortune.

Many types of industrial location are to be found, from relatively cheap land on Staten Island accessible to both rail and water, to fabulously expensive lots in lower Manhattan. The larger plants, especially those handling heavy materials like foundry and machine products, were established along the hundreds of miles of water front in the Bronx, Brooklyn, Queens, and Richmond, the greatest single area of concentration being around Newtown Creek that flows into the East River between Brooklyn and Queens. But the small plants of the clothing, fur, textile, jewelry, and other light industries sprang up originally, and stayed, on lower Manhattan, at the center of labor supply and close to their wholesalers. In order to control operations at a moment's notice, the newspapers have continued to print near their Manhattan offices. Many of the job printers have also found it desirable to stay near their customers. Other orientations to markets, cheaper land, or good transportation have scattered industry over the city; there is scarcely a square mile of Manhattan or near-by Brooklyn and Queens without some manufacturing establishment.

New York's workers have spread over more occupations and income levels than those of any other American city. Although no exact figures are available for all occupations, manufacturing in 1898 undoubtedly employed nearly half the working population. Wholesale and retail trade accounted for perhaps an additional quarter, while finance, personal service, professional service, transportation, hotels, and amusements made up the rest. The relative decline of manufacturing and the increase in trade and service activities substantially altered the pattern, until by 1940 the three major divisions each employed about a third of the workers.

These workers, including high-salaried executives, have lived under the most varied conditions. The poorest-paid group before 1900 had to put up with crowded, unhealthy tenements, the middle group lived comfortably in apartments or small homes in the outlying sections, and the highly paid executives had three or four-story brownstone houses. The next section of this chapter will discuss how government regulation

[158]

and subsidy improved the living conditions of tenement house dwellers. Our concern here is with the improvements of working conditions.

In the field of manufacturing, the clothing workers have steadily been the largest group, varying from a third to nearly a half of all those employed. At the turn of the century their working conditions were extremely bad. Russian, Polish, German, and Italian immigrants arriving without money or the chance to investigate American opportunities supplied most of the labor. The "putting-out" or contract system in many lines of the clothing industry made for competitive bidding by contractors and consequent pressure on wages. Rates were around 20 cents an hour and, as the demand was seasonal, periods of fourteen or more working hours a day, often at piece rates, were common. After these health-destroying periods of overwork would come slack seasons with weeks of unemployment and near-starvation.

Unionization offered a cure for these ills, but not an easy one. While the United Garment Workers and the United Hebrew Trades of New York were attempting organization in the nineties and the International Ladies Garment Workers Union after 1900, racial and religious differences among the workers and the large number of small shops and fly-by-night employers presented great difficulties. Until 1909 and 1910 strikes generally failed and membership remained low.

A strike at the plant of the Triangle Shirt Waist Company in September of 1909 started the spread of unionism. The beating and arrest of pickets aroused other clothing workers who flocked to a mass meeting, two thousand strong, at Cooper Union. A young girl, speaking in Yiddish, told of her beating by guards and moved for a general strike of all shirtwaist workers. Her speech created wild enthusiasm. Practically everyone present rose to second her motion, and the whole assembly with arms outstretched took the Jewish oath, "May this hand wither from the arm I now raise," to support a strike. Twenty thousand ultimately walked out, and the Women's Trade Union League, the United Hebrew Trades, the Socialist Party, and the Central Federated Union helped the ILGWU in organization and leadership. After almost three months of bitter struggle, in which liberal leaders such as Mrs. O. H. P. Belmont and Anne Morgan brought pressure to protect the strikers from continued brutality by police and armed guards, 337 firms gave in and settled with the union.

Later in 1910 a strike of 55,000 women's cloak and suit workers, backed by the ILGWU, resulted in a Protocol signed by employers and workers. Therewith the women's clothing industry established a new kind of unionism. The Protocol provided for the preferential shop, and appointment, by the employers and the union, of Joint Boards for Sanitary Control and Grievances. It also imposed restrictions on out-of-town contracts at less than union rates. In men's clothing the slow progress of the AFL United Garment Workers led Sidney Hillman and other vigorous progressives to organize in 1914 the Amalgamated Clothing Workers. Between 1915 and 1919 the Amalgamated established agreements with employers' associations in men's clothing similar to the Protocol for women's clothing. While agreements failed to end disputes in either branch, they marked the firm beginning of union strength and increasing order in the industry.

Some of New York's major industries, such as printing and metal work, were already unionized in 1898. The International Typographical Union, for example, was one of the oldest national craft organizations. In metal and foundry work several AFL crafts were solidly intrenched. But in many trades, em-

ployers resisted unionism as vigorously as had the dress manufacturers. In the building trades a strong employers' association
held off effective unionization for many years, but finally gave
way in 1910. By 1916, out of about 1,400,000 workers in the
city, 464,000 had joined AFL unions.

The company union first appeared in New York City in
transportation. In 1916, the Amalgamated Association of Street
and Electric Railway Employees of America, which had been
trying, without permanent success, to organize traction workers, called a series of strikes on Manhattan and Bronx subway,
surface, and elevated lines. The Interborough Rapid Transit
Company that operated the subways and, through its subsidi-
aries, a large part of the surface and elevated lines, responded
by forming the Brotherhood of Interborough Rapid Transit
Employees, a company union that, until 1925, prevented the
success of outside organizers.

From 1920 to 1948 the history of organized labor in New
York City was much the same as in the rest of the nation. The
American Plan, a strong employer drive against the closed shop
and union contracts in general, succeeded, during the depression of 1921 and 1922, in breaking the strength of many unions.
The East Coast Maritime Unions struck, lost, and sank into
insignificance. The new chemical and electrical industries
avoided unionization. But the well-established organizations
in the construction and printing trades held their own, and
the longshoremen, organized during the war, preserved their
new union.

The Amalgamated, in the men's clothing industry, held its
position through increasing cooperation with management,
but its development of better shop methods greatly reduced
the number of jobs. The ILGWU dwindled under both internal and external pressures, for, despite national prosperity, jobs

"DEFEND AMERICA" RALLY, MADISON SQUARE GARDEN, 1941

disappeared. The reasons were twofold: workers were being
supplanted by increasingly efficient machines, and women were
buying—and wearing—fewer clothes. Moreover, the ILGWU
itself, torn between Communists and moderates, was unable to
present a united front to employers. As a result, its membership had fallen from 100,000 to 32,000 by 1929.

The downswing of the business cycle from 1929 to 1933 de-
moralized unionism throughout the country. Membership fell,
and hard-won gains had to be abandoned in order to hang
onto jobs. The effect was particularly severe in New York's
leading industry. The efforts of the clothing unions to spread
employment kept absolute joblessness from mounting to more
than about 15 percent, but wages declined to the old sweat-
shop levels when out-of-town rates as low as 21 cents an hour

[163]

forced workers to join their employers in secretly undercutting union rates in order to stay in business.

The New Deal legislation completely changed the American labor scene. Section 7-A of the National Industrial Recovery Act of 1933 gave protection to union organizers and forced employers to bargain collectively with organizations representing a majority of their employees. Following the overthrow of vital sections of this law by the United States Supreme Court, Democratic Senator Robert F. Wagner from New York City introduced and helped to pass the Act that became the foundation of modern union strength. The Wagner Act of 1935 reaffirmed the provisions of Section 7-A and virtually prohibited employer efforts to coerce workers or to form company unions. Protected by this law, labor organizations grew at an unprecedented pace. The secession from the AFL by leaders favoring industrial unionism and the formation of the Congress of Industrial Organizations in 1938 added competitive intensity to the union campaigns. Meanwhile the industry codes of the NIRA and the partial recovery of business had done away with the worst phases of price-cutting in New York's largest industry and made it possible for the ILGWU and the Amalgamated Clothing Workers to enter into new and binding agreements with the employers.

Effective organization of white-collar workers had started with the Newspaper Guild for reporters and editorial employees in December of 1933, but the spread of organization among workers with middle-class traditions was slow. Up to 1937 unionism in New York City and elsewhere was largely confined to industry and transportation, and comparative wage rates showed the effects. Whereas clothing workers by 1939 were receiving $40.62 for a 32½-hour week, office workers in the city averaged only about $31 for a 35 to 38-hour week.

The formation of the CIO gave an added impetus to white-collar unionism and World War II established it on a secure basis in department stores and in many other areas of wholesale and retail trade, and in scattered sections of publishing, social work, and other professional fields.

Over the fifty years, as a whole, unions played a leading part in raising wages and reducing hours in most New York industries. While conditions in other city trades at the end of the nineteenth century were probably not so bad as in clothing, long hours and relatively low pay were the general rule for everyone from manual laborers to clerks and salespeople. The ten-hour day and the six-day week were the normal standard, and the average weekly pay envelope had less than three-quarters of the purchasing power of the pay received for a forty-hour week at the end of the nineteen thirties or in the years after World War II. Reduction in hours came about gradually. The widespread granting of half a day off on Saturdays was a gain of the first decade of the century, a reduction from ten to nine hours a day was generally achieved in the nineteen twenties, and the five-day week of eight-hour days was a result of the depression of the thirties. The forty-hour week was made the legal standard by a Federal Act of 1938.

Greater New York has become famous as the only place in the world where they erect great skyscrapers and then tear them down a few years later. Changing patterns of fashion and trade and increasing population led to this continual building and rebuilding. There is no way of estimating the real value of the gigantic mass of stone, wood, steel, and plaster, but assessed property values rose from some $3,000,000,000 in 1900 to $14,000,000,000 in 1946. Three major forms of building—offices, apartments, and one or two-family homes—accounted for most of the increased value.

The skyscraper has been the most expensive, spectacular, and unique building development. In 1898 the tall structural steel building, an American creation, was only about ten years old, and the tallest office buildings were boxlike structures of about twenty stories. The Singer Sewing Machine Company and young architect Ernest Flagg were responsible for the first of the great towers of Manhattan. Flagg, who had already won fame as a tenement-house reformer as well as for designing the Corcoran Art Gallery and the Naval Academy, made use, for the first time, of the great heights possible with steel construction. His 612-foot, 47-story Singer Building, begun in 1905, was almost twice as tall as it nearest rival. Thus was launched a thirty-year period in which great companies commissioned architects to design taller and taller buildings. The advertising and rental value accruing from the title of "World's Tallest Building" passed in succession to the 657-foot Metropolitan Tower, by N. LeBrun & Sons, in 1909; the 767-foot Woolworth Building, by Cass Gilbert, in 1912; the 1,046-foot Chrysler Building, by William Van Alen, in 1929; and finally, perhaps for all time, to the 86-story, 1,248-foot Empire State Building, by Shreve, Lamb and Harmon, in 1931. The last of the great skyscrapers prior to 1948, the Rockefeller Center group, represented a new departure in planned space. John D. Rockefeller, Jr., through his Rockefeller Center Incorporated, made the huge investment necessary to buy up the leases and demolish nearly all the buildings between Fifth and Sixth Avenues from 48th to 51st Streets. On this land, leased for 21 years from Columbia University with renewal clauses running to the year 2015, they erected, under the guidance of several architectural firms, fourteen tall buildings flanking a 70-story, 850-foot central monolith. The whole project cost over $100,000,000 and carried a mortgage of $65,000,000, held by the Metropoli-

WOOLWORTH BUILDING   *Wide World*   FLATIRON BUILDING   *Wide World*

tan Life Insurance Company. Even before its completion in
1940, the Center (also called Radio City) had become one
of the most attractive spots in the Greater City; and it was

soon a financial as well as artistic success. By 1947 the mortgage had been reduced to $30,000,000. Upon completion of the main Rockefeller Center buildings, Manhattan had nearly 100 buildings over thirty stories in height, and some "experts" were calculating that on the highest-priced land no new building of less than sixty stories would pay for itself.

Other "experts," however, recognized the problem as far more complex than the relation of the individual building to the cost of its lot. The long-run return to the investor was influenced also by the type of use for which the building was intended and by external conditions such as traffic congestion. While a financial district might maintain its values fairly well in spite of overcrowding, a trade area, with its need for deliveries and ready access by buyers, was far more vulnerable. Congestion in an artifically narrow zone, such as that between Seventh and Lexington Avenues in the mid-town section, would inevitably result in a gradual abandonment that might diminish existing property values. In fact, such overcrowding had been an important factor in reducing the highest assessments in the Wall Street area, between 1909 and 1926, from $22,500 per front foot to $22,000, while those in the newer 42d Street region had climbed from $12,000 to $24,000. Furthermore, in some areas the needs of trade placed such a premium on the rental of the street floor of a building that an inexpensive low building, even on the highest-priced land, might pay the best rate on total capital invested.

Such considerations combined with recognition of the need for stabilizing land value through preventing uses that unduly deteriorated the worth of surrounding property led the Board of Estimate and Apportionment, in 1913, to authorize the study of these problems. An able Commission, with lawyer Edward M. Bassett as Chairman and such veteran building reformers as Laurence Veiller and George B. Ford as members, submitted a comprehensive report in favor of regulating building heights and establishing "use districts." After a subsequent report on zoning by a smaller committee, also headed by Bassett, the Board, on July 25, 1916, adopted a building-zone resolution that marked a new American approach toward urban planning. For purposes of use the city was divided into three classes of districts: residential, commercial and unrestricted; for the regulation of height of buildings it was divided into five classes ranging from those on which buildings could not exceed the width of the broadest street on which they faced to those in which they might rise to two and a half times the street width. A Board of Standards and Appeals was also created by the state in 1916, and was subsequently given power over changes in zoning. Builders desiring to go beyond the maximum height could do so by setting the face of the building above that point back from the property line so as to conform to certain specifications laid down in the zoning regulations. This restriction produced the skyscraper with "setbacks" rising to a slender tower that has become the most impressive architectural feature of Manhattan.

During the rush hour, downtown and mid-town skyscrapers, holding ten to fifteen thousand people on lots of an acre or less, could be filled and emptied only by continuous streams of subway trains leading off in all directions. Manhattan, with a total resident population of under 2,000,000, by 1930 had about 1,500,000 daily workers, the great majority of whom reached their work by subway. Urban rapid transit was responsible, in general, for the enormous rise in land values in the early twentieth century. Competition for the choicest locations in skyscraper areas raised assessed valuations as high as $30,000 a front-foot in the case of Number One Wall Street or 500

Fifth Avenue. But rapid transit raised values in the outlying sections proportionately even higher by providing ten-cent commutation to the heart of the city. Whereas Manhattan land assessments rose 160 percent from 1905 to 1929, those in Queens rose 1,000 percent.

Until 1930, the gradual northward movement of business that reached a natural stopping point at 59th Street greatly enhanced land values along its line of march. High-grade retailers, hotels, financial institutions, and the central offices of big business occupied the most vaulable sites and were largely responsible for boosting property values. But when big business and finance moved into an area such as that around Grand Central, they brought with them lawyers, advertising agencies and all the other auxiliary services that were able to pay high rents for office space, and these specialists, in turn, bid prices up still higher. Like all real estate development the year-to-year movements of price were subject to sudden fads and to general booms and recessions. Shrewd operators made fortunes in mid-Manhattan by short-term buying and selling. George C. Boldt of the Waldorf, for example, bought the southeast corner of 37th Street and Fifth Avenue in 1901 for $1,200,000. Two years later he sold the property to Tiffany and Company for $2,000,000. The early twentieth century boom of the Times Square area doubled the value of surrounding real estate and made fortunes for other dealers in leases and lots.

Fashionable residential property also underwent violent fluctuations in price. The movement of the richest citizens in the late nineties to Fifth Avenue facing Central Park, and the development of Park Avenue north of Grand Central in the second and third decade of the present century, raised property values enormously. The southern rim of each of these residential areas shaded off into high-priced business districts.

PARK AVENUE

Wide World

But no given location is as valuable for even the highest-priced residential uses as for big business. No sane apartment-house builder of 1929, for example, would have paid $16,000,000 for the end of a block as did the Empire State Corporation. Devouring mansions and apartment buildings, business slowly encroached upon Park Avenue north of 45th Street and eliminated private houses from Fifth Avenue below 59th Street.

While the great operators made front-page news with their multimillion-dollar deals, contractors and development companies were steadily buying and building in the newer parts of the city. Each new trolley, elevated, or subway connection touched off a real estate boom. Up to the nineteen twenties builders generally laid out rows of nearly identical small houses on blocks adjacent to the new transportation facilities, but from the twenties on they built an increasing number of apartments. While one and two-family houses remained much more numerous than apartment buildings in every borough except Manhattan, only in Queens and Richmond have these small units continued to house a majority of the population.

The concentration of almost half the city's population in 1900 on landlord-owned Manhattan Island made the average New Yorker a rentpayer. Even the rapid spread of population to the other boroughs in the twenties, when Queens population grew by 130 percent, made only about 20 percent of New York's citizens homeowners. Most of the renters since the mid-nineteenth century have lived in more or less crowded apartment houses officially referred to as multiple dwellings or tenements.

In 1900 New York City had 82,652 tenements, largely on Manhattan Island, built in accordance with the inadequate provisions of nineteenth century housing laws. The six-story "dumbbell" tenement, so called because of a small interior court between buildings on 25 by 100-foot lots, was the common type of housing for the working class. Blocks on the lower East Side solidly filled with such buildings, which occasionally

HELL'S KITCHEN

were as large as seven stories and a basement, were the world's most crowded urban area. Thirty such blocks averaged over 1,000 residents per acre, or a rate of 640,000 per square mile. This represented the most economic use of the land in the eyes of the owners, but it was highly undesirable from the standpoint of public health or social welfare.

Aided by the writings of journalist Jacob Riis and architect Ernest Flagg, the movement for tenement-house reform gained strength in the nineties, but the legislation of that decade was largely ineffective. Finally, alarmed by the further deterioration as additional thousands of immigrants flooded in and old buildings decayed, reformers like Robert W. de Forest and Laurence Veiller secured more adequate action from the State Legislature. The Tenement House Act of 1901 is a basic statute in American, as well as New York, building reform; New York tenements built prior to that time are called "old law," those since the Act, "new law." The Act placed restrictions on the use of lots, regulated window areas, imposed strict fire regulations, required toilets and running water in each apartment, and provided for enforcement through a Tenement House Department. Existing buildings had to be remodeled to conform with certain parts of the carefully worded regulations. It took a decade, and still more regulations, to make the Act effective, but ultimately it eliminated the worst evils of the old slums.

The Act, however, had its bad effects. No new building conforming to the law could offer rentals as low as those in the existing tenements. In fact, as time went on and building costs rose, it became clear that new apartments could not be rented for prices within the reach of even skilled laborers. As a result, 67,000 old-law tenements were still standing in the middle twenties, and those destroyed had made way for business or

STUYVESANT TOWN, LOWER EAST SIDE, UNDER CONSTRUCTION

for middle-class apartments rather than homes for workers. For the average worker a move to Brooklyn, the Bronx, Richmond, Queens, or New Jersey seemed the solution of the problem, but at the cost of much time lost in travel and excessive congestion of the transit system. With immigration restriction from 1921 on, however, the pressure of new poverty-stricken foreigners for shelter diminished, and the poorest living quarters became less crowded. By 1925 the maximum East Side congestion had fallen from 1,000 to a little over 500 residents per acre.

The temporary housing shortage after World War I directed public attention to housing in general, and slum clearance became part of a broader movement for city planning. In 1921 the Russell Sage Foundation appointed a committee under the chairmanship of architect Frederic A. Delano to prepare a regional survey of New York. Meanwhile, Editor Wood and other publicists were writing on the problem of better housing; the *Survey* and other magazines were giving much attention to it, and British and German experiences were being studied.

The activities and writings of the planners and the support of the movement by Governor Smith won state and municipal recognition of the need for special encouragement for low-cost housing. The New York State Board of Housing, established in 1926, offered tax exemption to the securities of limited-dividend housing companies. The following year New York City provided 21-year tax exemption for projects of the State Housing Board. But these Acts had relatively little effect on the slum problem. In limited-dividend housing based on state and municipal tax remission (such as Knickerbocker Village on the lower East Side, finished in 1934) the rents were too high for manual workers. It was the need for made-work in the depression that moved urban slum clearance from planning to reality. The National Industrial Recovery Act of 1933 gave the Federal Government authority to spend money for "low-rent housing and slum clearance projects." Several local committees went to work immediately to insure New York City its share of the funds, and on February 17, 1934, Mayor La Guardia created a Municipal Housing Authority, with Tenement-House Commissioner Langdon W. Post as chairman.

The initial project, organized by the city and assisted by Federal authorities and known as the First Houses, was completed in May of 1936. From this time on, low-rent housing under municipal, state, or Federal direction was continually being constructed, until by 1944 thirty-one groups of buildings had been completed, and a considerable number of low-income residents had been rehoused.

WILLIAMSBURG HOUSING, BROOKLYN

While members of the middle-income group have seldom had to live in tenements, those bringing up families have suffered from lack of space indoors and light and air outdoors. In the late thirties the decline of interest rates on its other investments led the Metropolitan Life Insurance Company to initiate investment in adequate middle-class housing. Parkchester, a series of garden apartments in the Bronx, was the Metropolitan's first venture. Covering 129 acres and housing nearly 40,000 people, it was completed in 1940. In 1943, under the State Redevelopment Companies law, Metropolitan acquired eighteen blocks by condemnation and erected thirteen-story apartment buildings in place of the existing tenements. While the buildings, fully occupied, would more than double the population of the former East Side slum, their greater height allowed 75 percent of the ground area to be used for drives and gardens. Metropolitan and some of the savings banks are building additional developments of this type.

The dominant position of New York City financiers in the economic life of the nation from the nineties to World War I is connected particularly with the careers of three men: J. Pierpont Morgan, Sr., James Stillman, and George F. Baker. Each of these headed a great banking institution, and all three cooperated with one another and with lesser Wall Street giants to provide a uniquely positive and concerted leadership of national finance. Of the triumvirate, J. Pierpont Morgan, Sr., head of the great private banking house at 23 Wall Street, was the leading figure. Born to commercial and investment banking, this big taciturn man, with a manner so assured and an eye so penetrating that few men dared stand up to him as equals, assumed a new degree of responsibility for the conduct of the companies he financed and for the money market as a whole. While in those days there was no sharp line between houses selling securities and those doing commercial banking, Morgan's power came largely from his ability to market enormous blocks of securities at home or abroad. James Stillman's importance, on the other hand, came from the leadership of the nation's largest commercial bank. The National City Bank of New York had the largest deposits, both from local business and from out-of-town banks, the nearest approach, outside the Treasury, to a central gold reserve, and a dominant position in the market for United States Government securities. The First National Bank of New York and its president, George F. Baker, represented a small but important group of old and wealthy private and corporate investors, who kept large deposits in the bank and provided a select market for new securities.

The personal friendship and close financial cooperation of these three men, the forceful, aggressive Morgan, and the more cautious Stillman and Baker, in some ways provided a substitute for an American Central Bank. But, whereas a Central

WALL STREET, 1898

[179]

Bank might, like the later Federal Reserve System, have been controlled from Washington and have operated through several branches, the Morgan-Stillman-Baker "system" centralized control and operation in Wall Street. Boston, Philadelphia, and Chicago finance became more definitely dependent on New York than in previous generations, and this concentration of financial power applied to insurance as well as banking.

From the standpoint of total assets or rate of growth, life insurance, in the eighteen nineties, had already become the most important type. In the early years of the twentieth century the four largest life insurance companies, New York, Metropolitan, Mutual, and Equitable, were all located in New York City, but by 1909 Prudential of Newark had become third largest. At that time these five companies had seven and a half billion dollars of insurance in force, and assets of two billion dollars. By 1946 the four giants of the New York area—Mutual having become relatively smaller—had $79,600,000,000 worth of policies and $23,094,000,000 in assets. Among these big companies Metropolitan and Prudential differ from the others in having made special efforts to sell small policies to workingmen. This "industrial" insurance has, in turn, given them a special interest in public health programs. Haley Fiske was a leader of Metropolitan from the nineties until 1929. If he had been able to get the insurance laws altered, he would have worked out a complete plan of private social insurance from cradle to grave, and possibly given a different political turn to the later development of social security.

The rapidly growing life insurance assets offered the best market for the new securities of investment bankers, and consequently Morgan and Baker, particularly, became stockholders and directors in the biggest companies. By the time of the panic of 1907, when Morgan led the financiers of New York to

THE WALL STREET BOMB EXPLOSION, 1920

put up cash to halt runs on certain banks, the system inspired
by him had matured. Partners or officers of the biggest New
York banking houses sat on the boards of railroad, public utility, and industrial corporations that periodically required
financing, and on the boards of insurance, trust, and banking
companies that could buy or place new securities. According
to the Report of the Congressional Pujo Committee in 1913,
representatives of J. P. Morgan and Company, the National
City Bank, the First National Bank, and the Morgan-affiliated
Bankers and Guaranty Trust companies held 341 directorships
on the boards of 112 of the biggest American corporations.
This rather loose and uncoordinated structure of financial
influence, referred to by the Committee as the "Money Trust,"

[181]

was not only a system for greater banker control, but also for greater New York City control over large spheres of national economic activity.

The death of J. Pierpont Morgan, Sr., in 1913, the Federal Reserve Act passed in the same year, and World War I diminished the influence of the old leaders of Wall Street. The Federal Reserve Act made cash and specie available to member banks in time of crisis without the intercession of a Morgan or Stillman. The war and its aftermath increased the security-buying public to such a degree that the smaller investment houses could form syndicates and readily dispose of large stock or bond issues. And the next generation produced no such forceful leader as the elder Morgan.

In the nineteen twenties New York superseded London as the financial center of the world. As seven years of general prosperity from 1922 to 1929 increased the incomes of city people all over the nation, more and more money flowed into Wall Street for investment in stocks and bonds. The big financial houses strove to make the most of their opportunities. Led by Charles E. Mitchell, the National City Bank and its security-selling affiliate, the National City Company, went in for direct selling to the investing public on a grand scale. Through a continuous series of mergers the Chase National Bank grew in size until by the early thirties its resources equaled those of the National City Bank. It also had a selling affiliate, Chase Securities Corporation. But these banking leaders of the twenties lacked the close cooperation of the days before World War I. In the strict sense there was neither leadership in, nor responsibility for, the runaway stock market.

Meanwhile, New York banking facilities appeared in many of the trade centers of the world. The International Banking Corporation, a company started by Haley Fiske and other bank-

THE NEW YORK STOCK EXCHANGE   *Wide World*

ing and insurance men back in 1902, soon established a score
of branches in Europe, South America, and Asia. At the time
of World War I, James Stillman and Frank Vanderlip bought
control for National City Bank and created many new branches
in Latin America. About the same time the Guaranty Trust
Company also established foreign branches, and American Express Company did banking in its world-wide agencies. By
buying American Express Company's foreign banking business in 1929, Chase became the chief competitor of National
City abroad as well as at home. These far-flung systems, centered in New York, were used almost entirely for the finance of
American trade, but they also created bases that may be used

[183]

for the supervision of internal foreign investment at some future time.

Perhaps the sober citizens of New York would sooner forget the notoriety of their stock operators in the late twenties: the great speculators like Jesse Livermore, the glittering foreigners like Ivar Kreuger, or the more daring utility tycoons. It may provoke little civic pride to remember how every village and small city all over the land contained investors whose chief attention was focused on Wall Street quotations, and whose dreams for the future depended on hopes of receiving checks for market profits from some one of the nearly two thousand brokerage offices that dealt on the New York exchanges.

Unquestionably many wise New Yorkers suspected at the time that too much of the nation's savings was coming to the city and simply staying there, translated not into new labor-employing projects, but rather into inflated values and expanded credits. But almost no one foresaw the destructiveness of the collapse that started in late October of 1929. It seemed incredible that rents would fall so low that mortgage interest on some of the city's largest buildings could not be met, that mortgage guarantee houses of sixty and seventy years standing should go utterly bankrupt, that the greatest erstwhile leaders of finance should be investigated and deposed as unfit for their responsibilities, and that the banks of the nation should be closed by Presidential order. But within four years all this had happened.

The measures of the New Deal designed to stimulate and at the same time to reform business undoubtedly weakened the coordination and power of the New York financial community. The divorce of security selling from commercial banking in the Banking Act of 1933 forced the withdrawal of the great commercial banks from investment banking and split the House of Morgan in two, leaving a moderately large commercial bank under the old firm name and a security house under the name of Morgan, Stanley and Company. The regulations regarding information and responsibility in prospectuses of the Security Exchange Commission Act of 1934 made new security buying safer for the public, but made selling more hazardous for the bankers. The Commission had the power to force competitive bidding for new issues and at the same time to prevent the successful bidder from using any of the old trading techniques for maintaining the market price while the securities were being sold. First the Commissioners and later the Governors of the Federal Reserve System were given the power to regulate margins on stock transactions. In addition, the Reconstruction Finance Corporation took over part of the large-scale money-lending function formerly exercised by the big New York banks. It is not surprising that the morale of Wall Street men sank in the thirties, and they gloomily talked of the transfer of financial power from New York to Washington.

Neither World War II nor the post-war inflation wholly revived the security business. New York perhaps kept its relative position as the trading center of the nation, but new capital issues produced small profits for the underwriters, and trading on the Stock Exchange remained but a fraction of the volume of the nineteen twenties.

While the investment bankers and the brokers, the mighty men of the twenties, adjusted themselves to lean times and less prestige, from 1939 on commercial banking and insurance prospered. Although the more decentralized nation is no longer controlled from New York to the extent that it was in the days of J. Pierpont Morgan, we have no reason to believe that the world financial supremacy of the city is in danger.

ROCKEFELLER CENTER: THE TIME-LIFE BUILDING

The Social and Cultural Scene

By MARGARET CLAPP

IN THE year 1898 there were three ways into Manhattan: by ship, by the Brooklyn Bridge, and by the Vanderbilt-owned New York Central Railroad. The last was the most rapid, and the least pleasant. A tale then current described a passenger who survived the jolting ride through the sewer-like tunnel and at last, begrimed and choking from the smoke of soft coal and the sickly odor of oil lamps, arrived in irate state at the old Central Depot on 42d Street. Emerging, he saw a cow pastured across the way on Depew Place (where the Biltmore Hotel is now) on what seemed to be railroad property. "So," he muttered darkly, "the railroad isn't the only thing around here milked by the Vanderbilts." Far more pleasant was the trolley ride from Brooklyn across the Bridge.

Most comfortable of all was the approach by ship; yet visitors rarely mentioned the breeze and the flying spray. They could think only of their first view of slender stone shafts incredibly rising out of the sea to pierce the sky. Sailing nearer, they could distinguish five massive skyscrapers at the southern tip of the low-lying island, looming over the lesser giants of the last decade, the tallest of them all, the twenty-six story World Building, its gilded dome flashing in the sun. If a few people damned the big buildings as the art of Mammon, if others quipped that whenever a street became too crowded,

HERALD SQUARE, 1898

the city just tipped it on end and called it a skyscraper, most
people were awed. Those skyscrapers were symbolic of the
strength and pride and driving ambition of New York.

Yet in many ways it was an ugly city. The slums were horri-
fying. If people were poor, be they Americans white or black,
or recent emigrants from Russia, Italy, Austria, or Ireland,
they knew only the slums—filthy streets edged with grimy-
windowed stores and endless rows of five or six-story "walk-
ups." There was no privacy in this world of unheated flats and
back-yard pumps and privies. Where more than six hundred
people lived on an acre, only a fortunate family had two rooms
to itself, one for sleeping and eating, the other for cooking and
the inevitable sewing or cigar-making that eked out a miser-

able livelihood. But when reformers had tried to curtail the sweatshops, judges had expostulated against forcing a man "from his home and its hallowed associations and beneficent influences to ply his trade elsewhere."

These slums stretched across lower Manhattan, uniform in crowded poverty, otherwise presenting as colorful a variety of language and custom as any polyglot port in the world. Here was a pocket of fighting, loving Irishmen; there, a neighborhood of cleanly Jews; elsewhere, compact settlements of Germans, Greeks, Slavs, and Bohemians, each with its own tongue, its own stores, its own beer gardens, saloons, or cafés. Caught between the slums of the Bowery and the Five Points was Chinatown, at Chatham Square and Mott Street, where pig-tailed, loose-trousered, floppy-shoed Orientals carried on pri-

BROADWAY, LOOKING NORTH
FROM CORTLANDT STREET, 1898

HESTER AND NORFOLK STREETS, 1902

TWENTIETH CENTURY SURVIVALS

vate feuds (the last big one ended in 1904 with a forty-course banquet) and impassively sold "bargains" to sightseers. Not far from their gaudily painted, lanterned shops was a region of dingy streets where the staccato calls of pushcart vendors mingled with the cries of bambinos and the gay brave music of the organ grinders. This was little Italy, north of Mulberry Bend, probably the unhealthiest area in town; at least the death rate was highest.

Yet people look back with nostalgia on the good old days. Some of them have forgotten the grimness and remember only the fascinating variety. Others, of course, never knew the slums. Fifty years ago well-to-do people lived uptown in the pleasant Murray Hill section or perhaps on lower Fifth Avenue (twenty

Brown Brothers

THE VANDERBILT RESIDENCE, 5TH AVENUE

feet narrower then than it is today). Those were the districts of attached brownstone houses fronted by flights of steep stairs, although apartment houses and even new-fangled apartment hotels were creeping in.

Farther up Fifth Avenue, between 50th and 80th Streets, was the world-famous millionaires' row, which consisted of block after block of enormous, expensive, lavishly adorned private mansions, far more imposing than one palace could be, designed by the New World's ablest architects for the New World's new nobility. Still other people lived in modest comfort in the suburbs above 72d Street, many of them on unpaved roads and near vacant lots which they used as gardens. To the north were even patchier developments: a colony of Sicilians on East 116th Street; the impressive new buildings

AT THE VAN PELT
HOUSE, BROOKLYN

Owned by The New-York Historical Society

CONEY ISLAND, 1898 AND 1948

to which Columbia University moved in 1897 on West 116th Street; new homes along upper Riverside Drive; squatters' cabins in the rocky hills and dales around 125th Street.

Four other boroughs became part of New York in 1898. Brooklyn, most important of them, had a population of one million to Manhattan's one and one-half million. There lived descendants of early Dutch and English settlers, and wealthy newcomers who had moved over to the fashionable Heights at the same time that the poor started surging out of the congested areas of lower Manhattan—that is, after the Brooklyn Bridge was opened in 1883. By 1898 Brooklyn, too, had rows of apartment houses and dense settlements of native and foreign-born, but it had far more room in which to expand. Beyond

WILKINS FARM HOUSE, BRONX

beautiful, hilly Prospect Park vast flatlands with only occasional habitations stretched to the long, unspoiled shore line and to Coney Island, New York's playground.

The other boroughs, in comparison, were junior partners. Space-hungry Manhattanites began their big push to the Bronx only in the nineties, when extensions of the elevated railroads made commuting feasible. Blockfuls of single-family attached and detached houses were constructed so rapidly that the borough, made especially attractive by its pleasure-grounds—Bronx, Van Cortlandt, Pelham Bay, and Forest parks—seemed to turn into a city overnight. Yet even in 1898 so little of it was developed that the average population was not much over three persons per acre. Richmond and Queens were regions of

KING MANOR HOUSE, JAMAICA

small towns, farms, and open country. Lacking sure and speedy transportation to Manhattan, they could not attract many workmen for more than an occasional picnic.

This city of New York, as difficult to describe as the elephant was for the blind men, beautiful and ugly, cosmopolitan and provincial, magnet to the ambitious and Sodom to the preachers, was then, far more than it is today, paradoxical. Perhaps the one safe conclusion is that here nothing material has been changeless except the ever-changing tidal rivers and the outlying bays.

Forty and fifty years ago Greenwich Village was the hub of creative America to which came the imaginative sons of Iowa, Kansas, Maine, and all the land. Moody young Frank Norris wrote part of *McTeague* in a Village boardinghouse. In that same house a little later, Willa Cather, managing editor of *McClure's,* tried her hand at poetry. Richard Watson Gilder,

Wide World

SIDEWALK ART SHOW, WASHINGTON SQUARE

Will Irwin, and Richard Harding Davis, whose sweet tenor rendering of "On the Road to Mandalay" delighted Mark Twain, were Villagers. So, a little later, were John Barrymore, James Oppenheim, and the two Westerners, Theodore Dreiser and Sherwood Anderson, who established workrooms on St. Luke's Place.

May and James Preston, the illustrators, belonged to the Village. Jo Davidson had a studio there that was to become famous. An astonishing array of painters were residents, John Sloan, George Bellows, and Jerome Bloom among them. There also lived the composers Varèse, Ruggles, and Salzedo. Edna Millay, straight from Vassar, came to Bedford Street to a red brick house not quite ten feet wide, where she wrote part of *The King's Henchman*. Some of her plays had their first appearance in the near-by Provincetown Playhouse, which earlier had been a stable. There, too, Eugene O'Neill, son of the theater and child of the Village, saw his first plays produced.

These people and countless others lived in a camaraderie that no one who was part of it can ever forget. Let one of them have a modest success or a bit of cash and all of them joined to celebrate. The favorite spot was the old Brevoort on Fifth Avenue and 9th Street. There, a plump, retiring little man was apt to dine—O. Henry, who described the Village setting in many of his stories. Early in the century, white-maned Mark Twain used to walk down from his home at 21 Fifth Avenue to the Brevoort, and Oliver LaFarge frequently stopped in. LaFarge had his studio on 10th Street and his glass workshops on the south side of Washington Square.

In time, however, too many Villagers became famous. About 1910 their Village was "discovered." Sightseers flocked in. Tea Shoppes and gift bazaars were opened. Restaurants advertised as the American Left Bank. In consequence, some artists moved away; others, remaining, avoided the curious. But the old Village was doomed. By the 1920s quaint houses on MacDougal Alley commanded good prices. Successful artists were able to remain in the still charming district, but the Village of talented youth disappeared.

Harlem, now a crowded part of the city, was a pleasant suburb fifty years ago. Negroes then were concentrated in Brooklyn and in "Black Bohemia," a desperate slum southwest of Central Park near the Tenderloin. The successful among them, men like Harry T. Burleigh, the composer, led the way to a better land by renting long-empty apartments which Philip A. Payton found for them above 130th Street near Fifth Avenue. Others followed, in spite of vigorous objections from the resident whites, until in 1910 there were three or four blocks to the new Negro community. Came the first World War, job opportunities in New York, mass migration from the South; and Negro Harlem boomed. By 1920 more than one hundred thousand Negroes were living there, and today that number has tripled.

A city in itself, with as much variety in population origins, economic status, abilities, and interests as lower Manhattan has, its history has been marked by overcrowding, unsanitary tenements, poverty, and disease. Playgrounds and more schools, the city's continuous effort to promote a saner attitude, and increasing opportunities for work have, in late years, brought some alleviation. Nevertheless, Harlem epitomizes the most difficult local problems which face New Yorkers today—be they white or black: the old problem of congestion which exists, also, in other parts of the city; the need for decent, inexpensive housing at a time when costs have soared; and the problem of resolving deep-rooted race prejudices.

Similar tales of change could be told of almost any part of

HARLEM

New York. Fifty years ago the financial center was on Wall Street; publishers were near City Hall on Printing House Square; the wholesale merchandise business stretched south of 14th Street; the best retail shops covered Broadway from 14th to 25th Streets, and above them, to 39th Street, were the theaters. Today the financial district is still on Wall Street, but most newspaper publishers have long since moved north. Most book publishers went uptown from lower Fifth Avenue to Fourth Avenue above 30th Street. In so doing they pushed out the antique dealers who, in turn, went north to Madison Avenue in the 50s. The wholesale merchandise business also moved north, to the West 20s and 30s. Department stores jumped to the East Side, then gradually worked their way up Fifth Avenue, crowding out the spacious galleries of the art dealers who then moved to the East 50s. Even the Great White Way shifted so that its former northern limit became its southern edge.

Millionaires' row disappeared to be replaced by luxurious apartment houses. Park Avenue, which was an area of cheap frame houses and forlorn lots bordering the open cut of the Central Railroad, now joins the East 60s and 70s as a center of fashionable residences. Foreign sections are fast becoming native sections. (More than one half of the New Yorkers of 1898 were foreign-born; today not three in ten are.) The Five Points has become a playground; the Bowery Bhoy is gone; even the Tenderloin is but a memory. Effective tenement house laws and social service agencies are largely responsible for the change. The pioneering work of the Russell Sage Foundation has been particularly important. Established in 1907 to improve social conditions throughout America, it has encouraged and financed in New York child and family welfare organizations, has aided in the development of the case

EXCAVATING FOR THE TIMES BUILDING, 1904

Museum of the City of New York
Wide World

THE GREAT WHITE WAY, 1937

work method and the training of social service workers, and in the 1920s gave funds for the Committee on Regional Planning in New York. "Beschooled and beserviced," as Theodore Dreiser expressed it, the lower East Side has lost, along with its color, much of its hopelessness.

The compressed and ever-increasing numbers of people in Greater New York have caused the relentless push northward, southward, eastward, upward. While all the boroughs have gained residents, the increases have not been proportionate. Manhattan, still the most densely populated borough, housed more than half of all New Yorkers in 1898, but now has less than one fourth of the total. Brooklyn took the lead in the 1920s and today has 2,800,000 people to Manhattan's 1,900,000. Perhaps more astonishing is the development that has occurred in the Bronx and Queens. In the last fifty years the percentage of the city's residents in the former has risen from less than five to nineteen; in the latter, from four to eighteen. Only Richmond, still awaiting sure, speedy transportation, remains small, with but 188,000 residents to the million and more in each of the other boroughs.

The transportation problem of Richmond suggests a major factor in the growth of Greater New York. At the turn of the century the only public conveyances were surface trolleys, a few of them still horse-drawn; hacks; and, in Manhattan, elevated railroads. Even so, congested streets, especially where wagons had to make deliveries, and a growing accident rate where pedestrians, trolleys, hacks, and the new steam locomobiles competed at street crossings, alarmed the city fathers. In 1904 Police Commissioner McAdoo took action. Three mounted police were stationed at intersections on Fifth Avenue to initiate alternating traffic. A "fool reform," some people called it, as they also called the rotary traffic system

THE HENRY HUDSON PARKWAY

New York City Department of Parks

THE GEORGE WASHINGTON BRIDGE

The Port of New York Authority

started at Columbus Circle in 1905 and the isles of safety provided elsewhere for pedestrians.

Meanwhile, in that first decade of the century, the elevated railroads were extended far into the Bronx. The Williamsburg Bridge added a second link to Brooklyn. The first subway was opened from the Battery to the Bronx, then penetrated into Brooklyn. The first Hudson River tunnel was completed by William Gibbs McAdoo, and the Queensborough Bridge was thrown across the upper East River. In the next two decades new branches of the subways were built —more links between the boroughs. The Holland Tunnel was opened; while, on the surface, streets were widened and repaved to bear the new automobiles and motor trucks. In the 1930s projects long under way were finally completed, among them the noble George Washington Bridge, the Lincoln Tunnel, the first elevated express highway, and the great La Guardia Field in Queens—which for all its magnitude was inadequate, so that the greater International Airport at Idlewild on Jamaica Bay in Queens was rushed to completion and opened to traffic in the next decade. The thirties saw, also, the end of an era, for elevated railroads were declared obsolete and razing was begun; buses replaced trolley cars on the streets; and private ownership of subways was terminated. Thereafter, public transportation was to be increasingly a public responsibility.

Today there are many ways to enter Manhattan and cross between the boroughs: by ship, by subway, over fourteen bridges, through three vehicular tunnels, on four railroads. New Yorkers who for fifty years have talked, rightly, about the noise, dirt, and crowds on their public conveyances might talk with equal propriety of the matchless saga of transportation.

[204]

"Are there arts worthy freedom and a rich people?"

In 1898 New Yorkers were talking about the new free Public Library. The city fathers had promised to erect a home for it on 42d Street and Fifth Avenue, as soon as they razed the old Croton Reservoir, which had stood on that site since before the Civil War. People hoped that the City Art Commission, just established, would see that the library building was a credit to New York. Probably it would, because Charles McKim, Daniel French, and Oliver LaFarge were members of the commission. So were the presidents of the Metropolitan Museum, the Brooklyn Museum, and the Public Library, all of them men of taste. Rumor had it that the Brooklyn Museum was planning to open a Children's Museum in a year or so; a splendid idea, to teach all children to appreciate art, an idea that the Metropolitan Museum of Art should copy. But if the Metropolitan did so, where could it house the branch? It was already so crowded that many of its collections

Wide World

THE BROOKLYN MUSEUM

could not be displayed. Obviously what it needed was another wing.

Theaters were doing a flourishing business, but no one expected any of this year's plays to equal *The Little Minister,* starring Maude Adams, Charles Frohman's hit of last season. Music, however, was unquestionably superb. Emil Paur, who had been with the Boston Symphony, was just starting to direct the Philharmonic Orchestra. Given his interest in the moderns, and Walter Damrosch's delight in introducing new composers, the keen rivalry of the Symphony Society and the Philharmonic had been expected; and it certainly was providing a stimulating season. As for the opera, this, if ever, was the golden age. Surely never had there been so many stars in one place as Maurice Grau brought to the Metropolitan. Jean de Reszke himself was star enough for a whole company. The novels? Westcott's *David Harum* was continuing to get enormous sales. Of this year's crop everyone talked about S. Weir Mitchell's *Hugh Wynne, Free Quaker,* Alfred Ollivant's *Bob, Son of Battle,* and Charles Major's *When Knighthood Was in Flower.* People agreed that they were delightful romances, but some of them were afraid that the new method in the *Bookman* of listing the best-sellers in "Uptown" and "Downtown" New York might boomerang. What if all of the publishers, and most of them were here in town, set their standards by the *Bookman's* lists? Whatever would become of real craftsmen like Henry James?

So went the table talk in 1898. Through it ran three clearly distinguishable interests—in pure creation itself, in preservation of the artistic and literary heritage, and in developing understanding of all forms of expression among average New Yorkers. Those three interests, each retaining distinct individuality, have continued for fifty years to cross and recross each other, sometimes clashing but more often cooperating, and in the process have shaped the cultural history of the city.

Few New Yorkers doubted, even before 1898, that the taste of the ordinary man was of utmost importance. How else account for the city's willingness to donate land and a building to the Metropolitan Museum of Art as far back as 1879? Or for its insistence in 1891 that the Museum be opened on Sundays so that the workingman could enjoy the treasures on his one free day, even though there were bitter protests about profaning the Sabbath? For that matter, how else account for the willingness of the Museum staff to continue the Sunday openings after the disillusionment of their first Sunday? On that unforgettable day people came, marveled noisily; handled and broke some of the exhibits; looked in vain for the sideshows; sociably ate their picnics on the stairs, and quite ignored the implicit suggestion of the absence of cuspidors.

If in 1898 anyone still doubted the importance of the people, he needed only to look at New York's newspapers. William Randolph Hearst, young and stiff-jawed, had bought the *Journal* just three years before and entered into blatant competition with Joseph Pulitzer—an ambitious undertaking, because Pulitzer had a staff of thirteen hundred people on the *World*, was already spending some two million dollars a year gathering news, and had made an enviable reputation for public service by his editorial "crusades."

Their contest was the talk of the town; not that "nice" people bought the *Journal* or even the *World*, except, possibly, just to see for themselves the cheap sensationalism, the lurid crime tales in bold, black headlines, the pointless comic strips, and the highly colored "scoops" that were being fed to the public. The older generation shook their heads and won-dered what the country was coming to. As a matter of fact, it came to war in 1898; and New York's yellow press deserves much of the credit or blame for that. "You furnish the pictures and I'll furnish the war," Hearst was reported to have cabled to Frederic Remington, the illustrator, then in Cuba. Whether or not a true story, that was the spirit which increased circulation, and circulation mattered in what was rapidly shifting from a literary craft to a highly capitalized industry.

Though mass-circulation journalism was here to stay, the "yellow" in it faded shortly after the war. This was owing in part to Pulitzer's distress at the vapid outpourings and his sense of responsibility for a high standard of journalism. The *World* became a truly great paper. It was also owing in part to the remarkable recovery of the moribund *Times,* once the young Tennesseean, Adolph Ochs, took charge. He cut his price to a penny to compete with Pulitzer and Hearst. With a side glance at them, he tucked a slogan at the top of his paper: "All the News That's Fit to Print," and advertised of the *Times:* "It Does Not Soil the Breakfast Table." Nor did it. Conservative in opinion and format, an independent Democratic newspaper that supported McKinley in 1900 and Taft in 1908, it soon was making a profit. On the Republican side, the *Tribune* which Whitelaw Reid had taken over from Horace Greeley was a redoubtable force.

Between 1900 and 1914 well-informed, conservative New Yorkers usually read the *Times,* the *Herald* (owned by James Gordon Bennett, Jr.), or the *Tribune.* Intellectual liberals read Rollo Ogden's *Evening Post.* Liberals of all ranks read the *World,* which, divested of irresponsible sensationalism, was under W. H. Merrill and Frank I. Cobb an enterprising gatherer of news and a fighting journal of great power, much admired by Woodrow Wilson. The vast number who liked spiced news took the *Journal,* or the *Daily News* until Frank Munsey bought it and killed it. In Brooklyn the *Daily Eagle,* which was admirably edited for a generation by St. Clair McKelway, had a large following. Other New Yorkers read still other papers, either of the English or foreign-language press. In 1910 more than fifty daily papers, and twice that number of weekly papers, were published in the city. Clearly the reading public was growing.

As the reading public expanded after 1898, so did the number of magazines that catered to less discriminating tastes. By the turn of the century the older monthlies of high literary standards, the *Century, Harper's,* and *Scribner's,* were losing ground to *McClure's,* the *Cosmopolitan, Munsey's,* and other new ten-cent magazines. The trend was accelerated in the pre-war years, especially when S. S. McClure serialized Ida Tarbell's *History of the Standard Oil Company,* Lincoln Steffens's *Shame of the Cities,* and Ray Stannard Baker's *Railroads on Trial.* Others of the new magazines carried similar exposure literature. "Muckrakers," Theodore Roosevelt called the writers. But people in New York and elsewhere bought these New York magazines. What did they care for the fine points of expression? The "cheap" magazines were alive; they talked the language of the direct, unsophisticated majority of New Yorkers, and of Americans generally; and they aired long-felt grievances of the little people.

Literary men, chatting in the Century or University Club, were apt to deplore the public's taste and wish that education were more widespread and effective. As a matter of fact, almost every group in the city, whatever their special interests, found themselves talking about the importance of education, if not often, because it was a dull subject, at least occasionally.

Parents looked on education as the open sesame and desired it for their children. But the vast majority of adults, having had very little schooling, were easily confounded by the problems that arose. When William Maxwell, the fighting Scotch-Irishman who was Superintendent of Schools, demanded "a desk and a chair for every child," they approved. Yet when someone jeered that Maxwell confused sitting with learning, they were less sure.

Sheer numbers, the constantly shifting population and the variety of languages spoken in New York homes hampered educational progress. Nevertheless, the gains were steady. Before the consolidation of the boroughs, when Maxwell was Superintendent only in Brooklyn, so much progress had been made that by 1896 a mere five thousand children were turned away from elementary schools for lack of space. To be sure, first and second grade teachers in Brooklyn had an average

ERASMUS HALL ACADEMY, BROOKLYN, 1903

CURTIS HIGH SCHOOL, STATEN ISLAND

of seventy-four pupils each, but excellent citizens told Maxwell that a good teacher could easily handle seventy little ones.

Upon the consolidation of the boroughs, Maxwell's record made him the obvious choice as first Superintendent of Schools in Greater New York. When he commenced his new duties, he found diverse school systems, especially in the towns scattered through Richmond and Queens, and he brought more uniformity. He knew that Brooklyn and Manhattan had insufficient elementary schools. His annual reports chronicle what he accomplished: 18,000 new sittings in 1899; 20,000 in 1900: 27,000 in 1901, and so on. He knew that Brooklyn had four high schools; that Manhattan and the Bronx were in a worse position with only three day high schools, not one of them more than one year old; and he persuaded the city to add greatly to that number. He found education limited to academic drills. He added physical and

[211]

manual training. He found teachers with little understanding of their work. He, and far more than he, John Dewey at Teachers College, helped teachers to clarify their purposes.

But the part of their school system of which New Yorkers had the most reason to be proud was their unique, free City College. In 1898 the College had already celebrated its fiftieth anniversary on 23d Street and was making plans to move to larger quarters on St. Nicholas Heights. Boys from private schools could go to City College, as well as graduates of the new high schools and students from the College's own free Sub-Freshman class. Similarly, after 1902, girls could get a regular college course at the old, free Normal College. New York possessed twelve other colleges at the turn of the century, of which it was also proud, although most of them were private institutions for the sons and "bluestocking" daughters of the well-to-do. Among them, besides Columbia, New York University, and Fordham, were Wagner College, placed on a magnificent site—including the old Cunard mansion—on Staten Island; Manhattan College, which overlooks Van Cortlandt Park in the Bronx; Adelphi, a coeducational college in Brooklyn; and Cooper Union, the free college established by Peter Cooper to train poor youths in arts and sciences.

While educators were improving the schools, other citizens were developing library facilities for the many people who wished to educate themselves. In the nineties New York had shockingly inadequate library resources for so large a city as it had become. Except for small, private reference libraries serving only members or properly recommended individuals, there was nothing but a poverty-stricken Free Circulating Library whose few books appealed chiefly to children and the semi-literate.

[212]

FORDHAM UNIVERSITY, BRONX

Wide World

The Staten Island Advance

WAGNER COLLEGE, STATEN ISLAND

The first step in correcting that condition came with the consolidation of the resources of three private groups, the Astor, Lenox, and Tilden Foundations, and their joint establishment of a new institution, the New York Public Library. But before the new Library could function properly, it needed a building. This the city agreed to donate, after members of the Library Board pointed out that New York spent on library work a niggardly $26.39 per 1,000 population, to $379 in Boston and $565 in Springfield, Massachusetts. While the building was being erected, John S. Billings, the first director, organized the collections in the old Astor and Lenox buildings, using the most up-to-date library methods, and doing his utmost to serve the public in the cramped quarters. Then, when the 42d Street building was completed in 1911, he moved the original collections, the thousands of volumes given or purchased since the nineties, the splendid Avery collection of prints, and countless other treasures into the luxurious quarters of the new reference center.

Another step, paralleling in importance the establishment of the reference library, occurred in this period. In 1901 Andrew Carnegie gave more than five million dollars for the building of library branches which would hold circulating collections, and the city agreed to give the necessary lands and to make annual appropriations toward the support of the Public Library's Circulating Division.

More colorful, more talked about, more selfishly inspired was a building not far from the Library—the Metropolitan Opera House. Millionaires, so the tale goes, disgruntled back in the eighties by the modesty of the old Academy of Music and the stubbornness of New York's old elite who refused to sell their boxes, determined to have a building where they, too, could sit in glory. So they built their House around two

Golden Horseshoes and used their first meeting in the new building to draw lots for the best boxes. But fire gutted the interior in the nineties, and not all of the stockholders would contribute to a second building fund. Those who would, arranged, this time, for just one Horseshoe, the Diamond Horseshoe, with boxes only for themselves.

As owners of the building, they leased it to the opera com-

THE "DIAMOND HORSESHOE," METROPOLITAN OPERA HOUSE   [215]

pany of Maurice Grau. An excellent showman, conceiving opera as a means of presenting stars rather than as a form of theater with a balancing of voices, Grau sought out world-famous singers and built programs around their capacities. Those were the days of the de Reszkes, young Antonio Scotti, Emma Eames, Melba, Lillian Nordica, Lilli Lehman, Emma Calvé—the Carmen of her time—Ernestine Schumann-Heink, and a host of others whose names are remembered today.

Grau's star system was profitable financially, for New Yorkers loved to see celebrities, but many musicians believed that the art of opera suffered. Then the Conried Metropolitan Opera Company won a contract with the owners of the building. On Conried's opening night, November 23, 1903, the diamonds in the Horseshoe blazed as never before, while the audience buzzed with talk of the new company, the new conductor, the new maroon seats and the gold décor, the new smoking room designed by Carrère and Hastings—and the new star. On that evening Enrico Caruso, the radiant-voiced tenor, made his debut in "Rigoletto," offering the first of his six hundred and seven performances at the Metropolitan.

But all was not to be smooth sailing for Conried. In 1905 he had labor trouble. The chorus, which had organized as an AFL union, went on strike for recognition of the union and more pay. For three days stars acted as fill-ins, until Samuel Gompers persuaded the chorus to go back to work in return for some concessions. Conried also had difficulties with the public. He gave "Parsifal" on Christmas eve, 1903, over the vain protests of the pious, for example, of the Rev. Dr. Burrell, who urged Mayor Low to intervene. In 1907 Conried committed a greater offense. After holding a semi-public dress rehearsal on a Sunday morning, he introduced "Salome" to New Yorkers. One reviewer, the next day, felt impelled to

[216]

write of "the moral stench with which Salome fills the nostrils of humanity." Others described the scene at the Opera House—the shock, the white faces, the early departures.

Conried had competition, too. In 1906 the irrepressible Oscar Hammerstein opened the Manhattan Opera House on 34th Street. Though limited to French opera, he offered such excellent productions with Mary Garden and John McCormack that New Yorkers crowded the building. Conried, discouraged and in ill-health, gave up in 1908. To replace him, the ownership company called Gatti-Casazza of La Scala. He brought with him the conductor Arturo Toscanini whose name soon was on every tongue, as New Yorkers marveled at the artistry of his interpretations.

Two years later, the Metropolitan arranged a merger typical of the times. It bought out Hammerstein at a large price and wrote into the contract a clause forbidding him to produce opera in New York for ten years. Then it completed what it had already started, a system of interlocking directorates of the Metropolitan, Chicago, Philadelphia, and Boston opera companies. It was helpful for finances, if not for music.

Symphonic music had a happier development in New York, perhaps because it was not the child of fashion. Its home was Carnegie Hall where, through the years, New Yorkers went for their loftiest musical entertainment, in the early days walking or driving north from the residential area to the large, imposing building in a quiet, outlying part of the city, in later years, speeding by subway or car southward to an unpretentious building in mid-town Manhattan.

Two orchestras, the Symphony Society and the Philharmonic, oldest in the United States and fourth oldest in the world, played regularly at the Hall. In the pre-war years, after Paur left, the Philharmonic Orchestra was directed by Wasily Saronoff, Gustav Mahler, and a host of brilliant guest conductors. In 1911 youthful Josef Stransky came as regular conductor and won immediate popularity through his interpretations of Brahms, Liszt, and Strauss. Meanwhile, the younger of the rivals, the Symphony Society, created by music-loving Leopold Damrosch, remained throughout this period under the direction of his energetic son Walter.

People said that Walter Damrosch was running true to type when he insisted in giving contemporary musicians a chance to learn by hearing their works performed. All the Damrosches were musical educators, no doubt of that, although only Frank Damrosch was one professionally. He was Superintendent of Music in New York's public schools, organizer of amateur choral groups, organizer and conductor of the Musical Art Society, successor to his father and brother as conductor of the Oratorio Society, and organizer and director of the Institute of Musical Art. Believing ardently that familiarity leads to understanding, and understanding to appreciation, he conducted, also, symphonic concerts for children at Carnegie Hall as far back as 1897, to which many New Yorkers today fondly acknowledge a debt.

And what of the interest in painting and sculpture? Peppery old General Louis Palma di Cesnola, erstwhile Garibaldi redshirt and for twenty-five years director of the Metropolitan Museum of Art, could talk about that. He had come to the city-supported museum back in 1879, to a small red brick building uptown in Central Park. Before his career closed, the red brick had been replaced by white Indiana marble, and, what was more significant, three large wings had been added to accommodate new donations.

In the decade prior to the outbreak of the war in Europe,

METROPOLITAN MUSEUM OF ART

during the presidency of J. P. Morgan, the Museum's acquisitions mounted even more swiftly. Sometimes it seemed that no treasures would be left in Europe, so rapidly were the old masters being shipped across the Atlantic, and so avidly were rich Americans seeking more. Having made their purchases, most multimillionaires, fortunately, wished to share the enjoyment of them, so that all of the museums of America profited, though none, perhaps, as much as the Metropolitan. There students came to sketch and dream among the old masters; schoolchildren came with their teachers; social New York drove up to inspect new donations from their friends, about which (and about whom) they would then talk at dinner; and in ever-growing numbers ordinary citizens came in to see and be refreshed.

Yet not everybody thought that the Museum was perfect.

[219]

Down in Greenwich Village there was grumbling: the Museum was too conservative; the Museum could not conceive of an artist being great unless he were dead; the Museum was doing nothing to educate New Yorkers to the beauty of modern art. Nor were the private art dealers any more helpful to Village artists. Purchasers wished traditional art, preferably by Europeans, and dealers did not dare give space to the showing of works by contemporary New Yorkers.

Gertrude Vanderbilt Whitney came to the rescue of the native artist in 1908 by establishing the Whitney Studio Gallery in the heart of the Village on 8th Street. There, in rotating exhibits, American artists working in New York, men like George Bellows, Robert Henri, John Sloan, Ernest Lawson, and Jo Davidson, were able to display their work.

All of them were realists. Robert Henri, for example, an Ohioan who had studied in Paris and came to New York in 1900 filled with the glories of Manet and Goya, was disgusted with the sickly sentimental pictures that some Americans painted and other Americans bought. "Do not imitate," was the motto in his art classes, and he himself lived up to it. Most of the younger, Paris-trained artists who used the Whitney Studio were derisively labeled members of the Ash Can School. They were savagely satirical in their honesty, painting the truth as they saw it, but, their opponents said, they could see truth only in slums.

In 1912 Village artists organized the Association of American Artists and Sculptors, and decided it was high time New Yorkers had some idea of what was happening in the modern world. So they collected works of their own and sent to Europe for works of their friends, especially of French artists. In 1913 they opened the doors to the International Exhibit of Modern Art—the Armory Show. New Yorkers came—

[220]

gasped; came again, and still gasping, stayed. It was unbelievable. They wandered among post-impressionism, modernism, cubism, utterly bewildered, looking for something that they could recognize. The colors were beautiful; the designs effective; but what were the pictures about? Probably no picture ever displayed in New York was as much talked of as Duchamp's "Nude Descending a Staircase." Newspapers on the whole were condemnatory, not only of that picture but of the whole show. Many of them ridiculed it, suggesting that perhaps the show had been hung upside down by mistake. But the young moderns who put it on did not care. They had opened the eyes of New Yorkers, and, they hoped, had ushered in a new era.

Meanwhile, the older, established artists had completed an era of beautifying the city. Foremost among them was Charles F. McKim of the architectural firm of McKim, Mead and White. When he began his career, public buildings were mainly of red brick; before he was through, they were of marble. He was responsible for the Municipal Building; the Brooklyn Institute of Arts and Letters; the General Post Office on Eighth Avenue on which is carved Herodotus' famous sentence; the Century and University Clubs; the Morgan Library; and the Pennsylvania Waiting Room, of which Arnold Bennett was to remark with admiration and humor that there everything could be found except the trains. Stanford White, his popular junior partner, made a unique contribution through his search for unity among the arts. He himself designed furniture, decorated a yacht for James G. Bennett, made magazine covers for *Scribner's* and the *Century,* and constructed pedestals for the sculpture of St. Gaudens. He renovated the Players Club, of which he was a member; designed the Washington Arch and the Prison

GOING HOME FOR CHRISTMAS, PENNSYLVANIA STATION   *Wide World*

Ship Martyrs Monument in Brooklyn; and, most important
of his works in the city, did the Madison Square Garden—a
fact New Yorkers recalled when later he was shot and killed
there.

The sculptors also made their contribution. Gentle Herbert Adams sculptured the statue of Bryant that watches over
Bryant Park. Brooklyn-born William Macmonnies made the

NEW YORK UNIVERSITY, HALL OF FAME

famous Nathan Hale standing in City Hall Park. Karl Bitter,
protégé of the architect Richard M. Hunt, made representa-
tions of Architecture, Sculpture, Painting, and Music for the
Metropolitan Museum of Art, and the finely conceived
Schurz monument on Morningside Heights. Daniel Chester
French sculptured the figures for the Manhattan Bridge,
others for New York University's Hall of Fame, and Colum-

[223]

bia University's "Alma Mater." Augustus St. Gaudens, laboring in his West 36th Street studio, sculptured the heroic Sherman placed at 59th Street and Fifth Avenue, the Peter Cooper in Cooper Square, and the Farragut that adorned Madison Square (it has been replaced by a granite replica). George Gray Barnard executed the "Pan" in Central Park. Many other artists, commissioned by private individuals, by civic and religious groups, and by the city itself, found opportunities in New York. That, possibly, explains in part the advice given to St. Gaudens in his younger days: "If you are not in New York, you are camping out."

The belief of later years that World War I killed one era and sired another seems hardly valid, at least in regard to cultural life in New York. Interest which New Yorkers had shown before the war in artistic creation, in preserving works of art, and in giving all citizens more chance to enjoy the arts and letters was quite as evident between 1920 and 1948.

Nor were the controversies between classicism and modernism which raged in the twenties other than a development, undoubtedly stimulated by the war, of issues already before artistic and literary New Yorkers. The Armory Show proved that. New Yorkers were still arguing its merits in 1914. Were these modern forms significant new departures or fads? It was too soon to tell, perhaps; yet it was worth noting that the most talented of the younger artists were their advocates. The fact that Edward Robinson, director of the Metropolitan Museum of Art, had bought a Cézanne for the Museum also caused talk. Though he had not given publicity to his purchase, might it presage a new attitude at the Metropolitan towards the moderns?

A hint of doubt even touched the complacency with which New Yorkers viewed their architectural gems. Of course, no

[224]

THE BILLOPP HOUSE, STATEN ISLAND

one could question the beauty and appropriateness of such monuments of the past as the Billopp or Conference house at Tottenville on Staten Island, built in 1677 in English colonial style; the Dyckman house, erected on Dutch colonial lines in 1783; Fraunces Tavern, where royal governors ate from 1719 onwards, and where Washington took leave of his officers at the end of the Revolution; the Lefferts mansion in Prospect Park, Brooklyn; and the handsome Jumel Mansion, constructed in 1765. But Victorian houses had a different quality. Artistic citizens were wholly pleased at the way Charles McKim had torn down the front stairs, renovated the brownstone fronts, and made tasteful ground floor entrances to homes. They were delighted with the beauty of their public buildings. And yet, out in Chicago, Frank Lloyd Wright was making interesting innovations. A few, a very few, New Yorkers thought that his emphasis on functional form and the beauty which he was creating through the simple lines of unadorned steel might be more suitable to an American city than Gothic skyscrapers and Greek-columned apartment houses.

The new currents had so affected literature not only in New York but across America that even the best-seller lists in the pre-war years hinted of the change. In the nineties writers of romances were all popular. They still were the most popular, but favorites like Churchill, McCutcheon, and Porter were joined occasionally by O. Henry, Upton Sinclair, and Somerset Maugham. Even more striking were the experimentation and honest approach of the younger writers. Much of their work appeared in the "little magazines" of the second decade, centered in Chicago; yet New York also had its share of these artists and also gave them a chance to be known.

The famous old publishing houses of New York, houses like Harper and Brothers, Charles Scribner's Sons, Dodd, Mead and Company, and G. P. Putnam's Sons, had not lived to celebrate their fiftieth anniversaries by ignoring new trends and new writers. Necessarily interested in authors whose books would sell, they were also eager to find young authors whose later books might sell. To be sure, they were not as receptive as the young writers wished; nevertheless, the attitude of the editors of the old houses had changed perceptibly within a ten-year period. Elizabeth Jordan, for example, coming to New York in the nineties and starting as a reporter on the *World*, became literary adviser to Harper and Brothers in 1913, where she helped to discover Sinclair

Lewis, Dorothy Canfield, and others. It was hard to believe in 1914, the year that *The Titan* was published, that just fourteen years earlier Doubleday and Page had published Dreiser's first novel, *Sister Carrie,* and then, fearful of it, had avoided circulating it.

Besides its world-famous publishing houses, New York had its "little magazines" where newcomers could get a hearing. Art Young, for example, who moved to New York early in the century, joined with Max Eastman and others to establish the radical and highly literate *Masses* (not to be confused with the later *New Masses*) in 1911. Equally significant in the world of letters was *The Seven Arts,* a monthly magazine which first appeared in November, 1916. James Oppenheim was the editor, with Waldo Frank as associate editor and an advisory board that included Kahlil Gibran, Louis Untermeyer, and Van Wyck Brooks. "We are living in the first days of a renascent period," the editors wrote in the summer of 1916. "It is the aim of *The Seven Arts* to become a channel for the flow of these new tendencies; an expression of our American arts which shall be fundamentally an expression of our American life. We have no tradition to continue; we have no school of style to build up. What we ask of the writer is simply self-expression without regard to current magazine standards."

The Seven Arts immediately attracted thoughtful, and fervent, writers of the time. In the one year of its existence Sherwood Anderson published in it two of his Winesburg stories. Paul Rosenfeld, recently from college, sent in some excellent musical criticism. Young Randolph S. Bourne contributed a number of strong essays indicting modern society. William Rose Benét and his brother Stephen, a student at Yale, sent poetry. Kenneth MacGowan and J. D. Beresford wrote for it; so did two men on the staff of the *New Republic* —Harold Stearns and Walter Lippmann. Of course the editors and the advisory board contributed, as did Theodore Dreiser and H. L. Mencken.

But before the conflict in America between modernism and traditionalism reached a climax, World War I started in Europe. Its immediate effect on the cultural life of New York was to curtail archeological research by the American Museum of Natural History and to end art collecting in Europe. It cost New York the presence of many of Europe's outstanding musicians who either chose to serve their homelands in the crisis or were caught in Europe by the suddenness of the outbreak. That had a fortunate side for American artists long struggling for recognition in their own country. So did the wave of patriotism which swept America upon its entry into the war and which left a backwash of intolerance that banned German opera and canceled engagements of German and Austrian artists. Willingness to hear Americans did increase. Thereafter, American artists in New York, both conservatives and experimentalists, felt able to compete on equal terms with European visitors. Even so, interest in native artists, as in modern art, had existed before the war and was merely accelerated by it.

Mention of the 1920s immediately recalls prohibition "speakeasies," jazz bands, easy money, and speeding cars; Mah Jong or a fevered discussion of a "quickie" on Freud one evening, and the next evening to the movies to see Rudolph Valentino. But those phenomena warrant comparison more with the barbershop harmony, the bicycling parties and charades, and the heated disputes about "the higher criticism" of an earlier decade. Similarly, the 1930s suggest depression, and the 1940s, war and inflation. Yet across the changing decades New York had a vigorous artistic and literary movement, comparable to the pre-war period, though more equally concerned with modern and traditional forms.

Among musical champions of the moderns, Walter Damrosch was preeminent as pioneer and persistent advocate. In the post-war period he commissioned the versatile Deems Taylor to compose "Jurgen" which the Symphony Society performed. More startling was his approval of young Brooklyn-born George Gershwin. In 1924, Gershwin, aged twenty-six, worked at top speed for ten days and turned out "Rhapsody in Blue" which Paul Whiteman's orchestra performed in Aeolian Hall. Conservative circles were affronted by this merging of popular and concert music. But not Walter Damrosch. The following year he invited the young man to compose a piece for his orchestra, and the "Concerto in F" had its première in Carnegie Hall. Two years later, as enthusiastic as he had been forty years before over the latest music, the sexagenarian introduced his audience to Gershwin's catchy "An American in Paris."

Similar encouragement to modern composers came from the Philharmonic Orchestra, the New Symphony Orchestra organized in 1919 to play modern music only, and the Manhattan Symphony Orchestra conducted by Henry K. Hadley from 1929 to 1932, in which time he introduced thirty-six American works. The Metropolitan Opera Company, which had presented its first American opera in 1908, paid increasing attention to contemporary American music in the twenties and thirties, performing, for example, John Alden Carpenter's radical, cacaphonic "Skyscrapers," New York-born Deems Taylor's scores of "The King's Henchman" and "Peter Ibbetson," and Louis Gruenberg's score of O'Neill's "Emperor Jones."

The shifting currents of opinion affected painting and sculpture no less than music. Private art dealers lost their fear of modern art and gave contemporary Americans numerous opportunities to exhibit their work. Therefore, considering its original function achieved, the Whitney Studio Galleries closed, and in their place was created the Whitney Museum of American Art on West 8th Street, in 1931. Living artists, new talent as well as established Americans, were, and are today, represented in the Whitney's permanent collections and in frequent loan exhibits.

Meanwhile, a Museum of Living Art was established in the Village, and in 1929 the Museum of Modern Art was founded through the patronage of Mrs. John D. Rockefeller, Miss Lillie Bliss, and others. International in scope, devoted primarily to the work of the last fifty years, the Modern Museum on West 53d Street rapidly built collections of painting, sculpture, architectural designs and models, industrial arts, theater arts, photography, and films. Today its collection of twentieth century art is considered the most representative in the world. Its film library, an extraordinarily rich collection of some eighteen million feet of film, is itself evidence of the Museum's orientation in the modern world, and is an invaluable source for historians as well as artists. Fully as important have been the loan exhibits at the Museum, of which the Van Gogh show in 1935 was perhaps the most impressive. Over 140,000 New Yorkers visited it, and when it went on tour some 800,000 Americans saw it.

The triumph of the moderns extended beyond music, painting, and sculpture to architecture, and to the theater and other literary forms. Functional architecture appeared in New York in the 1920s, most characteristically in the clean-lined skyscrapers. The theater experienced a renaissance, as if dramatists and poets, too, would strip away out-moded convention and irrelevant trivia. The Provincetown Players, who had for several years made the Village their winter headquarters, and the Washington Square Players who developed into the Theatre Guild in 1919, found Broadway critics and enthusiasts coming downtown to see the work of the young writers and actors. Foremost of their discoveries was Eugene O'Neill. In 1919 his "Beyond the Horizon" won the Pulitzer Prize, as his "Anna Christie" and "Strange Interlude" did in the twenties, and as his work as a whole, especially the three plays of the early thirties, all produced by the Theater Guild—"Mourning Becomes Electra," "Ah, Wilderness," and "Days Without End"—earned for him the Nobel Prize for literature in 1935.

Other dramatists, seeking a richer, more honest theater, rose to prominence in New York between the 1920s and 1940s; necessarily in New York, for Broadway is the path to prominence in the American theater. Some of them were born New Yorkers—O'Neill, Sidney Kingsley, Elmer Rice, Moss Hart, Clifford Odets. If a few seemed to think New York was thrust upon them and tried to avoid the city, far more of them became New Yorkers, as, for example, Maxwell Anderson, Rachel Crothers, Robert Sherwood, Zoë Akins, S. N. Behrman, Marc Connelly, and George Kaufman.

Among these people of diverse interests, new directions led to experiments in scenery, and in no scenery; in realistic conversational pieces, and in dramatic recitals; in hard-hitting exposure of social weaknesses, reminiscent of the muckrakers, by men like Odets and in the Federal Theater directed by Elmer Rice; and also in a lofty poetic prose and blank verse treatment not only of tragic themes of the past, but of contemporary tragic themes, as in Maxwell Anderson's "Winterset," which he labeled "an attempt to establish a new convention."

The 1920s also saw the continuation of *The Smart Set,* a magazine started in 1917 and edited by George Jean Nathan and Henry L. Mencken. Provocative, zestful, its goal was to free literature from the bondage of convention. Among its contributors were F. Scott Fitzgerald, George M. Cohan, Aldous Huxley, and James Branch Cabell. Another important magazine begun in the 1920s was Henry S. Canby's *Saturday Review of Literature,* which soon became and is still a foremost vehicle of literary criticism. Meanwhile, the old *Nation,* brilliantly written, never smart, continued in the early twenties to excel in literary and dramatic criticism, while the *New Republic,* first issued by Herbert Croly and others in 1915, had a wide audience among young intellectuals.

Yet with so much energy devoted to creating a new tradition in all the arts and in letters, interest in conserving the old persisted unabated. Consider the museums in the last thirty years that have maintained and are today maintaining a traditional course or a primary concern with the past. The Metropolitan Museum of Art's Egyptian expeditions, commenced in 1906, have produced the largest, most representative Egyptian collection in the United States; and its Persian expeditions, started in the 1930s, have already been rewarding. The Museum itself now extends for four blocks along Fifth Avenue and welcomes some two million visitors a year —sufficient evidence to prove its importance to New Yorkers. It displays extensive Greek and Roman and Far Eastern collections, as well as others from Egypt and the Near East; it has a section of decorative arts, of arms and armor, and an American Wing. All that is in addition to its main attraction, the superb picture galleries.

In recent years the Metropolitan's work has extended far beyond its walls to bring collaboration among the city's museums. In 1943 it made a coalition with the Whitney which provided for eventual housing of the Whitney in the Metropolitan and for allocation of funds by the Metropolitan to enlarge the Whitney Museum's modern American collections. So, in time, the whole history of art in America will be represented in one place in a way that will conserve the tradition and encourage new developments. In 1947 other consultations led to a clear division of function between the Metropolitan and the Modern Museum by which paintings owned by the latter will be sold to the Metropolitan as time passes and they are no longer modern, while the Museum of Modern Art will use these funds to add more recent works to its collections. Another and quite different coalition took place in 1947 when the Metropolitan allied itself with the Costume Institute, which then moved into the Metropolitan, in order to make available to students, designers, and manufacturers their combined resources.

Among other museums which help to conserve and display the heritage are two long-established institutions, one city-assisted, the other private, and both equally free to the public. The former is the Brooklyn Museum, founded by the Brooklyn Institute of Arts and Letters in 1897. Wholly modernized in the 1930s, this Museum is today noted for its excellent primitive collections and its happy balance of classic and modern works of art. The latter museum is the New-York Historical Society, established in 1804, and now located on Central Park West. Also rebuilt and very much enlarged ten years ago, it has excellent facilities for showing its rich collections of Americana, especially relics of New York.

A museum particularly fascinating to New Yorkers is the

THE MUSEUM OF THE CITY OF NEW YORK   *Wide World*

Museum of the City of New York. Miniature groups depict
scenes in New York city history. A whole room is devoted to
fire engines and fire-fighting across two centuries. Elsewhere
are displays of old toys, costumes, furniture, and even whole
rooms from old New York houses. Paintings, prints, and
documents tell the story of famous New Yorkers. Miniature
works of art by such people as the Archipenkos, Carl Sprink-
horn, and Clagget Wilson are on display, as well as exhibits
relating to the theater and opera to which Charles Frohman,
Geraldine Farrar, and other artists have contributed. Incorporated in 1923 and housed at first in the Gracie Mansion,
the Museum moved in 1932 to its own home on Fifth Ave-

[235]

nue at 103d Street, on land given by the city and to a building paid for by public subscription.

On East 36th Street is the Morgan Library, established in 1924 to display the works of art, books, and manuscripts of J. P. Morgan. On Fifth Avenue at East 70th Street is the Frick Museum which was opened in 1935 in the house designed by Carrère and Hastings for Henry Clay Frick. Supported by funds left by Mr. Frick, this museum, filled with superb paintings, tapestries, and furniture, is free at all times, for the purpose of "encouraging and developing the study of the fine arts." Because it has the atmosphere of a private house, it has the rare opportunity of showing in appropriate surroundings the relations between the arts of one time and place, as in the Fragonard Room. The most recent of New York's museums is likewise housed in a former Fifth Avenue mansion. That is the Jewish Museum, the first of its kind in the United States, located in the former Felix Warburg home at 92d Street. Opened in 1947, it shows representative works of Jews of the past and present to illustrate the history and continuity of the Jewish tradition.

Far uptown is the Cloisters, perhaps best known of New York's newer museums. Before the first World War George Grey Barnard, the sculptor, accumulated medieval architectural pieces and examples of Romanesque and Gothic sculpture which he housed in delightfully informal style near his studio. But it was too costly for him to maintain, and in 1925 he sold his pieces to the Metropolitan Museum of Art, to which John D. Rockefeller gave the funds for the purchase. It was then decided to erect for the collection a special building, to be called the Cloisters, in Fort Tryon Park, which Mr. Rockefeller had given to the city. Combined efforts of Charles Collens, the architect, Joseph Beck and James J.

THE CLOISTERS, FORT TRYON PARK

Wide World

[237]

Rorimer of the Metropolitan, and Mr. Rockefeller, who also paid for the building, resulted in a structure so simple that it never detracts attention from the exhibits, and so in keeping with medieval architecture that the original pieces which are incorporated into the design, especially the Cuxa Cloister, are enhanced.

Some of the city's historic dwellings are also preserved as museums or shrines, among them the Lefferts homestead in Prospect Park, Brooklyn, the Edwin Markham home on Staten Island, Van Cortlandt House in the Bronx, Chisholm Mansion in Queens, and the Poe Cottage in Fordham. These and other similar shrines in the five boroughs present to visitors a gracious evocation of the social and literary life of an earlier day.

Like the art museums, scientific institutions have steadily enlarged their offerings, and like most of the art museums they have been aided in their work by city gifts of land and buildings. The Botanical Gardens in Bronx Park and in Prospect Park have become places of beauty as well as centers for scientific study. Similarly, the Zoological Gardens in the Bronx Park, in Brooklyn, and on Staten Island give pleasure and provide opportunities for research.

Most important, oldest, largest of all New York's scientific institutions is the American Museum of Natural History, "a bed-rock establishment," as it says of itself, "which rests squarely upon basic schist one billion years old." Its twenty-three acres of building on Central Park West are at once a museum, a laboratory, a school, a publishing house, and headquarters for exploring expeditions. Scientists plan the trips, conduct them, bring back their findings; analyze, classify, and relate their discoveries to other knowledge; publish the results of their investigations; and prepare exhibits from some of their new materials for the display halls of the

IN THE BRONX ZOO

museum. Among the most famous have been the North Pacific Explorations undertaken at the turn of the century and, supported by Morris K. Jesup, long president of the museum, for the purpose of seeking racial, cultural, and historical connections between North America and Asia; the expeditions of Carl Akeley in Africa, in which Theodore Roosevelt took part and which resulted in African Hall; and the Central Asiatic expeditions into the Gobi Desert which Roy Chapman Andrews, later director of the Museum, began in 1918. Many others, too many to mention—for some years find as many as fifty or sixty explorations in progress—have been of similar importance to science.

From explorations and gifts have come collections of dinosaurs and birds, which are the finest in the world, and anthro-

[239]

pological collections which are among the most complete. Once the exhibits were merely identified and classified. Now they are planned with a larger view in mind, to depict all forms of life in their native environment and in their various stages of evolution; while, close by, studies of other planets are promoted in the Museum's Hayden Planetarium, opened in 1935. When funds permit, new arrangements of the materials, only one-fifth of which are on display for casual visitors, will further the Museum's lofty aim—to show man a "conception of the Cosmos and his place in it." This new plan, for which Director Albert E. Parr is largely responsible, will have a hall of comparative anatomy; a hall dealing with the physiological foundations of human and animal behavior; another showing the origins and spread of material culture; and other halls which will review the nature and development of civilization in specific areas.

Scientists, it would seem, cherish the discoveries of the past, while pushing forward advanced research in the present. Publishers issue and reissue the classics, as well as contemporaries. Theaters continue to present Shakespeare and ancient Greek plays, in one guise or another, at the Theatre Guild, or in Eva LeGallienne's Repertory Theater, or at one of the regular houses. So musicians play the moderns, and yet continue to interpret the masters as devotedly as ever. Indeed, never in New York's history have the classics been read with as sensi.ive awareness of their full meaning as in recent times. For Arturo Toscanini came back to New York after the first World War. He had left the Metropolitan Opera Company in 1914, refusing to lower the quality of his performance to aid an economy drive. When he returned, it was not to the Metropolitan, however; that phase of his career was closed. Instead, he was a guest conductor and then associate con-

[240]

MAYOR LA GUARDIA AND CONDUCTOR WALTER

ductor of the Philharmonic Orchestra. In 1928, when rising costs threatened the financial existence of symphonic music, the two old rivals, the Philharmonic and the Symphony, joining their resources, formed the Philharmonic-Symphony Society; and Toscanini became its conductor. For seven years the slight, trim, temperamental master held his orchestra to unparalleled efficiency and his audiences to the most careful attention. He was succeeded by John Barbirolli and Artur Rodzinski, and today Bruno Walter maintains the high symphonic traditions.

[241]

Efforts to arouse public enthusiasm and to educate average New Yorkers in letters and arts have multiplied most astonishingly. Admittedly the new tabloids, notably the *Daily News* and the *Mirror,* which battled in the 1920s as crassly as the yellow press of the 1890s, cater to uneducated tastes. Admittedly the *Evening Post* lost all its intellectual prestige when Cyrus H. K. Curtis took it over, and it has become the tabloid *Post.* The *World,* despite the able leadership given it by Walter Lippmann, Herbert Bayard Swope, and others, perished in 1931—a heavy loss to the city. Moreover, Frank Munsey slew the *Press* and the venerable *Globe and Commercial Advertiser,* distinguished by its brilliant staff. He bought the old *Sun* of Dana, merged it with the *Herald,* and sold the combined newspaper to the *Tribune.* The *Times,* under a succession of able editors (Charles R. Miller, John Finley, Rollo Ogden, Charles Merz) has pursued a path of increasing usefulness and power. The *Tribune* has taken on greater influence, greater perhaps than at any time since the days when Horace Greeley's opinions were read and discussed throughout the nation. The Brooklyn *Eagle,* completely reconciled to the changes which marked the creation of the Greater City, still remains a center of Borough affection and civic pride. In the Bronx, the well-edited *Home News* has become an important daily. The Negro press is represented by three capable weeklies with rapidly expanding circulation. In addition to these newspapers, the museums, the music, dance, and theater groups, the publishing houses, and, to a degree, the new medium, radio, have made remarkable strides in popularizing the best traditions as well as modern trends.

Today New York's educational facilities are overburdened. Over 818,000 children attend the 732 schools. More than 60 percent of them are in elementary schools; 22 percent are in academic high schools; about 12 percent are in the junior high schools; and 5 percent are in vocational high schools. Formal academic instruction and physical training are carefully maintained, and activity programs are being expanded. Science, art, and library exhibits are brought to the schools, in projects arranged by teachers and leaders of city-supported museums and libraries. Nor do the children remain fixed at their desks. Each year thousands of them are taken to visit the zoological and botanical gardens and other New York institutions. For example, they spend a day at the American Museum of Natural History under museum guidance, and another at the Metropolitan Museum of Art or at the outstanding Children's Museum in Brooklyn where they can handle exhibits specially prepared for them. In their free time many of them return to the museums or join storytelling groups at their local libraries. Some of them attend the Young People's Concerts of the Philharmonic-Symphony Society, long conducted by Ernest Schelling and more recently by Rudolph Ganz.

QUEENS COLLEGE

BROOKLYN COLLEGE

More opportunity for higher education exists today than was dreamed possible only a few years ago. The city's free colleges have some 67,000 students, of whom more than 18,000 are in the day sessions. Only about 45,000 of them are in City College and Hunter, however, for two more colleges have been added to the city system in recent years: Brooklyn College, established in 1930, and already second largest of the free colleges, and Queens College, established in 1937. Both of them are coeducational institutions housed in attractive, if overcrowded, brick or stucco buildings on pleasantly landscaped campuses, one in Flatbush, the other in Flushing. In these four colleges the ambitious and ablest high school graduates can qualify for bachelor's degrees, and commencing in 1948 may take a five-year course in teacher education. In three of them, City, Brooklyn, and Hunter Colleges, graduate courses leading to the master's degree are offered.

Nineteen private colleges and universities in New York also give broad programs of higher education. The most important of them is Columbia University, one of the distinguished educational institutions of the world. In addition to

[244]   HUNTER COLLEGE   COLLEGE OF THE CITY OF NEW YORK

COLUMBIA UNIVERSITY IN 1898

Columbiana

three undergraduate schools, it has a graduate school, a law school, a medical school; schools of architecture, music, journalism, engineering, and business; and still other important divisions. Nicholas Murray Butler, president for forty-three years in this century, worked tirelessly to develop the present physical plant, breadth of offerings, and strong faculty. Acting-President Frank D. Fackenthal initiated some important new policies; and in 1948 Columbia looked forward to the beginning of another era of progress under its new president, General Dwight D. Eisenhower.

Eminent scholars on the faculty of Columbia and on the staffs of the other colleges in New York, both free and private, are active leaders in the city's cultural life. Some of them are connected with the science and art museums; others work with charitable and educational foundations in the city; still others are distinguished artists as well as teachers of the arts. Today, as in the last few decades, a large part of the writing by New Yorkers in the humanities, arts, and sciences stems from these intellectual centers.

Almost all of the institutions of higher education also offer courses for adults who wish to continue their education but who are not qualified or are not interested in seeking formal degrees. Particularly active in this respect is the New School for Social Research, established by James Harvey Robinson and others in 1919, and its University in Exile, which Alvin Johnson added in 1934, where distinguished refugee scholars lecture.

Yet institutional efforts to serve future leaders and to reach a mass adult audience are not limited to the schools and colleges. The three free library systems of New York are important to millions of its citizens. The Brooklyn Public Library has a modern central building which is an excellent example of contemporary architecture, thirty-six branch buildings, more than one and one half million volumes, and a circulation of about five million volumes. Yet the Brooklyn Library is dissatisfied. It knows how dilapidated some of its branches are, and how much more service it could give with larger appropriations at its disposal. Commenting on the three cents per capita which the city gave it for books in the first year after World War II, the director noted: "Of course, one could not buy comics for King's County at such a figure." Similar problems and similar achievement are evident in the Queens Borough Library system, which today has a central building, eighteen branch libraries, and approximately 800,000 volumes.

The New York Public Library serving Manhattan, the Bronx, and Richmond, is much the largest and most important. The Circulating Division has sixty-five branches with a total circulation, each day, of enough books to make a stack

BROOKLYN PUBLIC LIBRARY

two and one half times as high as the Empire State Building. The Reference Library, to which more than three million people come each year, is second only to the Library of Congress. Scholars from all the world consult its collections, and profit from talks with department heads who are experts in their fields. Musicians, artists, industrial designers, as well as casual readers find assistance in getting the material which they wish. Library statistics show that members of the staff answer thirteen million reference questions a year, many of them queries coming in by phone. Yet, like the other libraries, the New York Public Library is handicapped by insufficient funds, both in the city-supported circulating division and in the privately endowed reference division. Impressively large though its collections are, it has, in fact, only two volumes per borrower in comparison to eleven per borrower in Boston.

REFORMED DUTCH CHURCH OF FLATBUSH, BROOKLYN

Another, and most pervading, force for enriching the lives of New Yorkers stems from the religious institutions of the city. New York has hundreds of churches and synagogues, some of them dating from the seventeenth century, some of

[248]

them built in the last decade. They represent a wide variety of beliefs: Roman Catholic and Greek Orthodox; all the Protestant groups, including the Episcopal, Methodist, Reformed, Presbyterian, Lutheran, Congregational, Baptist, Seventh Day Adventist, and Christian Science; and Religious, Conservative, and Reformed Jews. Most of them are neighborhood centers vital in the lives of parishioners, but modestly housed in buildings unknown to New Yorkers at large. Many of them, however, are far-famed for beauty, size, or historical importance.

Brooklyn, "City of Churches," has several old establishments. The Flatbush Reformed Protestant Church dates from the late eighteenth century, its first building having been erected under the direction of Peter Stuyvesant. Another early church is the Episcopal St. Ann's, called the Mother of Churches because six churches have stemmed from it. Long familiar have been the old Church of the Pilgrims where Dr. Richard S. Storrs was serving in 1850 and still served in 1898, and the Plymouth Congregational Church where the militant abolitionist, Henry Ward Beecher, and then Lyman Abbott (editor, also, of *The Outlook*) attracted national attention. Those two churches united in 1934 to make the Plymouth Church of the Pilgrims. In the twentieth century Dr. S. Parkes Cadman made the Central Congregational Church famous, through his dynamic radio sermons and his work as part founder and one-time president of the Federal Council of Churches of Christ in America. Almost as well-known in Brooklyn are the Roman Catholic Church of St. Teresa, which has more than fifteen thousand members and a parochial school of two thousand children; and the Tompkins Avenue Congregational Church, the largest of its denomination in the country.

CHURCH OF SAINT ANDREW, RICHMOND *Staten Island Institute of Arts and Sciences*

Among the older religious centers in the Bronx are historic St. Ann's, where generations of the famous Morris family are buried, and Temple Beth Elohim, housed in the old home of Richard M. Hoe, inventor of the rotary printing press. Staten Island also has long-established churches, one of the best known being the Episcopal Church of St. Andrew, where Samuel Seabury, first American bishop, once served. Even older are two churches in Queens: the gray-shingled, hipped-roof old Quaker Meeting House, erected in 1696, and the

RIVERSIDE CHURCH

ST. PATRICK'S CATHEDRAL

First Presbyterian Church, which lays claim to being the oldest Presbyterian congregation in America, though its present building dates only from the early 19th century.

In Manhattan the best known of the old churches is probably the Episcopal Trinity Church in the heart of the financial district. About as familiar to New Yorkers are the beautiful Church of the Ascension on 10th Street, the Church of the Transfiguration ("The Little Church Around the Corner"), the Church of the Holy Cross—where Father Duffy, Chaplain of the "Fighting Sixty-Ninth," served—and the Fifth Avenue Presbyterian Church, which has had a long line of able leaders of the caliber of John Henry Jowett.

Most of the large religious denominations have central

[251]

Wide World

Wide Wo

CATHEDRAL OF ST. JOHN THE DIVINE   TEMPLE EMANU-EL

establishments in Manhattan. The noble Roman Catholic Cathedral, St. Patrick's, is at Fifth Avenue and 50th Street. There Archbishop McCloskey presided in 1898, and after him John M. Farley served, first as Archbishop, then as Cardinal, to be followed by Cardinal Hayes and Cardinal Spellman. Erection of the Episcopal Cathedral of St. John the Divine on Morningside Heights was begun in the 1890s when Henry Codman Potter was Archbishop of New York, and displays today the work of foremost New York sculptors and architects, especially the designs of Ralph Adams Cram. At Fifth Avenue and 65th Street is Temple Emanu-El, oldest Reformed synagogue in New York, which merged in 1927 with Congregation Beth-El and moved to its present building

[252]

in 1929. Uptown is the Riverside Church, which was opened in 1929 and which through the leadership of Dr. Harry Emerson Fosdick won immediate repute for its community and interdenominational activities.

Most of the religious groups of New York have extended their activities far beyond the walls of their buildings. Some of them have established settlement houses, orphanages, and clinics. Particularly notable in this respect is the work of frail Mother Frances Xavier Cabrini, who came from Italy to work among Italians in Manhattan and the Bronx, and who, becoming a citizen, remained to found some seventy charitable and educational institutions in America before her death in 1917. Mother Cabrini became the first American to be beatified. Other leaders have worked outside the old denominations. Felix Adler, for example, was founder and long the leading spirit in the Society of Ethical Culture. The Salvation Army, directed in New York in the 1880s by Ballington Booth and his wife, was later led by Frederic Booth-Tucker and then by Evangeline Booth, after the Ballington Booths had resigned from the movement in the 1890s to found the Volunteers of America. More recently Father Divine in Harlem has combined religion, morality, and low-cost food and lodging houses.

Countless other individuals and religious groups deserve mention as living proof that New Yorkers are not wholly materialistic. It is true that many New Yorkers have departed from the orthodoxy of their fathers, and many others are irregular attendants at religious services, yet the role of New York's churches and synagogues in establishing standards, in guiding conduct, and in improving city conditions has been and remains one of utmost significance.

New York publishers of magazines, newspapers, and books

are also making important contributions to cultural life. News magazines with enormous circulation, like phrase-provoking *Time,* cover artistic and literary developments. Other magazines, which present condensations of thought on all sorts of subjects, popularize a wide variety of ideas. Picture magazines like *Life* bring expert photography and reproductions of great works of art, as well as information, to vast numbers of people. Newspapers, particularly the *Times,* the *Herald-Tribune,* and the Brooklyn *Eagle,* which are read by ever larger numbers of New Yorkers, give whole sections to discussions of literary, artistic, and scientific news. Book publishers offer inexpensive editions and paper-backed pocket books which make many classics as well as some contemporary literature and light fare available to everyone.

Music and theater are within the reach of average-income groups. Museums in the city regularly sponsor free musical programs. At the Lewisohn Stadium, which offers popularly priced outdoor concerts, as many as twenty thousand people gather on a summer evening to hear the Philharmonic-Symphony Society. The City Center of Music and Drama, with a price scale ranging from $2.00 to $.30, attracts thousands of New Yorkers each year. Just five years old, it was established after block-size Mecca Hall fell to the city in default of taxes and no one made a satisfactory bid for it. The city thereupon decided to use it to help New Yorkers enjoy the arts. It now rents it for a nominal sum merely equal to taxes to a non-profitmaking corporation, the City Center of Music and Drama, Inc., on an experimental basis, to see if low-price, high quality art for large audiences can be self-supporting. There New Yorkers hear the New York City Symphony Orchestra which Leopold Stokowski organized and which Leonard Bernstein has been conducting, the New

York City Opera Company under Lazlo Halasz, the New York City Theater Company directed by José Ferrer, and visiting companies like the Ballet Theatre and the Ballet Russe.

But radio is the truly revolutionary factor. In 1910 Lee de Forest arranged to broadcast a performance of Caruso in "Cavalleria Rusticana" from the Metropolitan Opera House. Wireless operators on ships in New York harbor, newspapermen gathered in de Forest's Newark factory, a few men in another room in the Opera House—all told, about fifty people—heard the program. "One or two of them thought they heard a tenor," the New York *Sun* reported. "They were not positive. They all did hear a constant tick-ta-ta-tick." Despite the scoffing, the possibilities of radio for mass entertainment and education seized imaginations. Since then, so stupendous have been the strides in wireless technology that today radio is a reliable, common or garden variety of convenience, and television is the exciting new medium with which New Yorkers are getting acquainted.

The national networks, NBC, ABC, CBS, and MBS, have their headquarters in New York, in or near the seventy-story RCA Building in Rockefeller Center, where eleven floors, sound-proofed, air-conditioned, filled with delicate and exact instruments, are set aside for studios ranging in size from tiny rooms to a hall seating thirteen hundred people. The city also has a radio station, WNYC, which it has owned and operated since 1924. It broadcasts music from City Center, Carnegie Hall, Town Hall, the Lewisohn Stadium, and other New York halls. It presents local news, messages from city officials, health and educational talks, and world news. Interested in encouraging American artists, WNYC holds an annual American Musical Festival in February, emphasizing

American music and new American talent. Morton Gould, Leonard Bernstein, and Paul Bowles are among the many American musicians who were first heard during these city-sponsored festivals.

Listeners also benefit from the many radio forums, book programs, dramatic features, and most of all, from musical programs. The Metropolitan Opera Company broadcasts regularly, as it has since 1931. The result has been to give the opera a nation-wide audience that came to its support when bankruptcy threatened in 1940. Toscanini conducts the weekly broadcasts of the NBC Symphony Orchestra, as he has been doing for eleven years. The New York Philharmonic-Symphony Society estimates that some thirteen million people listen to its Sunday afternoon coast-to-coast hook-up. Gone are the days when it was fearful lest the new device "cheapen" music or lessen attendance at Carnegie Hall. Radio has so extended its audience of lovers of serious music that competition for seats at the Hall between natives and visitors has multiplied. In short, familiarity has bred affection.

An even wider circle of devotees is reached by the broadcasts of sporting events. During the first half-century of Greater New York's history, organized sport took on the attributes of big business enterprise. As the lines of distinction between amateur and professional became somewhat blurred, the spectator began to receive even more attention than the performer. New Yorkers sought their recreation in crowds, watching others in competitive play. In 1915 George L. ("Tex") Rickard took over the old Madison Square Garden, then full of the memories of P. T. Barnum's shows, and packed it with thousands of boxing enthusiasts who hoped to see a champion in the making. Within ten years Rickard and his associates had built a new Garden and had made it the metropolitan center of professional and semi-professional sport. But it was more than that. It gave direction to the perennial search for pleasure, in a generation which associated leisure with action. Boxing is only one of its attractions. There one might see spectacular hockey, with the Rangers battling the Montreal Canadiens for the Stanley Cup, basket ball tournaments, both professional and intercollegiate, skating carnivals with Sonja Henie, Western rodeos, horse and dog shows and the circus, brought indoors for the benefit of city dwellers who cannot enjoy the thrill of the "big top" in its traditional setting on the vacant lot.

International News Photo

JAMAICA RACE TRACK

THE YANKEE STADIUM *The New York Yankees*   EBBETS FIELD   *Brown Broth.*

In New York no spectator sport based on team play has seriously challenged baseball. Though the mounting attendance figures at Ebbets Field, the Polo Grounds, and the Yankee Stadium have not quite kept pace over the years with population statistics, there is no apparent decline in popular interest. The followers of Giants, Dodgers, and Yankees are as fiercely loyal to their respective teams as they were in the days of Christy Mathewson or "Rube" Marquard or Lou Gehrig. In the last thirty years New York teams have participated in eighteen World Series, and seven times the Yankees for the American League have taken the field against the Dodgers or the Giants, as pennant winners in the National

League. Every sport has its national heroes, but probably none has ever won greater fame than Babe Ruth in 1927, with his season record of 60 home runs. His influence on the youth of America reminded New Yorkers that baseball is socially significant, not because millions crowd the league parks, but because the small boy still marks out the diamond on vacant lots and municipal playgrounds.

In New York the spectator has almost, but not entirely, obscured the participant. Even track and field events, once staged in relative solitude at Mott Haven on the banks of the Harlem, now draw thousands. The completion of the Randall's Island Stadium in 1936 has given the city an excellent cinder track and a superb field for outdoor meets, such as the annual Labor Day Games. Here and on many smaller fields in the five boroughs the Police Athletic League, the Park Department, and the Public School Athletic League encourage team play and individual prowess. This is the city's best guarantee that the future will find those who play as well as those who watch at such events as the Millrose meet, the Knights of Columbus games, the tennis finals at Forest Hills, the Metropolitan Open Tournament for golfers, the intercollegiate football games and the diamond battles. On many a school playground or park field young New Yorkers are trying to emulate the records of Reiser, Di Maggio, and Robinson.

Looking to the future, it is safe to predict that the cultural and social autonomy of the boroughs will increase. Since 1923, Brooklyn has been more populous than Manhattan, while by 1940 both the Bronx and Queens were pressing the tight little island hard. With their own colleges, newspapers, department stores, museums, libraries, and parks, and with well-rooted cultural agencies with traditions and ideals of their own, the separate boroughs are certain to develop a healthy self-sufficiency in many fields. Politically, and to a considerable extent economically, Greater New York is a unit. In nearly every other respect it is a constellation of five stars, each one of which is proudly conscious of its own life, and eager to give it greater luster.

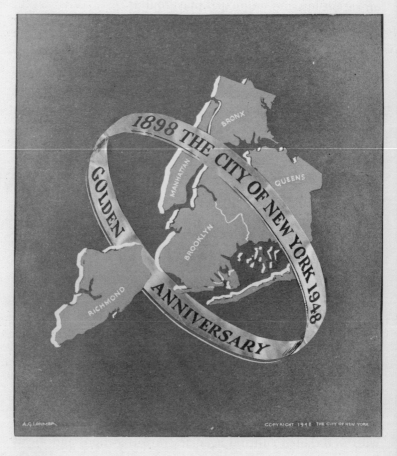